# Advance Praise for *You Are Beyond Belief*

"Find your inner faith, a faith derived from the verb Fidere which means To Trust. Jordan Paul is inviting us to trust again, ourselves and each other. The book is a pure delight taking you by the hand, by the soul inviting you to find your authentic, enlightened self. Open your heart, give wings to your soul and take a journey to the center of your existence."

—Emmanuel Itier,
humanitarian filmmaker of *We The People* and *The Cure*

"In a time when many frustrated people attribute their angst to others who are different or believe differently, a book filled with the light of the author's honest story of personal growth is a pearl on life's seashore of sand. I highly recommend this book to everyone in the world!"

—Pat Lynch,
founder & CEO, WomensRadio(R)

"A beautiful blend of innate wisdom, powerful storytelling and an encouragement to take a deeper dive into what and who we believe ourselves to be. Jordan Paul has lived a life of adventure, reflection and joy. He invites us to do the same."

—Cynthia James,
transformational coach and best selling author of *I Choose Me: The Art of Being a Phenomenally Successful Woman at Home and at Work*

"Beautifully written, *You Are Beyond Belief* is Jordan Paul's personal story of triumph over limiting beliefs that ultimately brought him to be able to embody his existence in a state of love. His story inspires and reminds us that we have the choice to look beyond the limitations of rigid belief systems (our own and those imposed on us by others), to trust our hearts, and to discover that we too have the power to exist in a state of love and positive beliefs."

—Eva Selhub, MD.,
author of *Your Health Destiny, The Love Response, Your Brain on Nature* and *The Stress Management Handbook*

"Written with deep vulnerability, we witness a lifelong quest devoted to following the path of a loving heart. This book inspires us to fully step into personal beliefs and choices that bring rich insight for an empowered and purposeful life."

—Carl Studna,
luminary photographer, inspirational speaker,
and best selling author of *Evolution of Loving*

"I have had great respect for Jordan Paul since the publishing thirty years ago of *Do I Have to Give Up Me to Be Loved by You,* a book which I still recommend to couples! Now I am delighted to endorse Dr. Paul's new book. Part personal reflection, part self-help, *You Are Beyond Belief* is full of practical tools to help the reader move from pain to joy and from fear to love. As the poet and spiritual teacher Rumi advised, "Your task is not to seek for love but merely to seek and find all the barriers within yourself that you have built against it." *You Are Beyond Belief* offers us a map and some personal practices to do just that."

—Debra Manchester, LCSW
executive director, Family Therapy Institute of Santa Barbara

"Once again, Jordan Paul has gifted us with an inspiring and most human gem that invites us to find their value in our own lives. Dr. Paul's easy-reading style is never preachy, but rather gently encouraging. No matter where you are in your own exploration, you will find this book a welcome companion."

—Jeff Grossberg,
CEO Guidestone Consulting

"A gift drawn from the many years of a very conscious person and psychotherapist. The idea of changing your limiting beliefs into evolving/empowering beliefs is quite original and very doable."

—Diane Mason,
award-winning journalist and filmmaker, founder of HOPE FILMS

"*You Are Beyond Belief* unites personal and professional insights to show how to turn our self-limiting beliefs into life-empowering beliefs. With inspiring vulnerability, he reveals his journey as a pioneering psychotherapist. Advocating an evolved balance of mind, heart, body, and soul for both women and men willing to become their true selves, Jordan Paul helps us see how our lives improve as we believe in the value of authenticity."

—Judah Freed,
author of *Making Global Sense*

"Exquisitely weaving the evolution of his own personal life experiences into an elaborately crafted set of empowering beliefs. Simply stated and easily understood, these beliefs allow the opportunity to incorporate them into one's own life journey. This incredibly open and honest self reflection is not only enjoyable to read but empowers each of us to experience the joy of staying connected to our heart, no matter the circumstances."

—Conrad Boeding, MA,
school counselor and author of *The Love Disorder*

# You Are Beyond Belief

## Breaking Free from Limited Thinking

Jordan Paul, PhD

Book Publishers Network
P.O. Box 2256
Bothell • WA • 98041
PH • 425-483-3040
www.bookpublishersnetwork.com

Copyright © 2019 by Jordan Paul, PhD

All rights reserved. No part of this book may be reproduced, stored in, or introduced into a retrieval system, or transmitted in any form, or by any means (electronic, mechanical, photocopying, recording, or otherwise) without the prior written permission of the publisher.

10 9 8 7 6 5 4 3 2 1

Printed in the United States of America

    LCCN  2019906450
    ISBN  978-1-948963-29-9

*Editor: Julie Scandora*
*Cover design layout: Launa Fujimoto*
*Interior design: Melissa Vail Coffman*
*Cover photo: Kai Kalhn/Pixabay.com*
*Jordan Paul Photo: Carl Studna*

{ Contents }

Chapter 1 – Personal Evolution:
The Never-Ending Journey toward the Possible You . . . 1

Chapter 2 – Emotional Evolution:
I'm Full of It and I Love It . . . . . . . . . . . . . . . . 7

Chapter 3 – Sexual Evolution:
Keeping My Heart On . . . . . . . . . . . . . . . . . . 25

Chapter 4 – Spiritual Evolution:
Living in the Mystery and Being Love . . . . . . . . . 43

Chapter 5 – Intellectual Evolution:
Being Smart Has Nothing to Do with IQ . . . . . . . 57

Chapter 6 – Career and Creative Evolution:
Finding Passion and Being of Service. . . . . . . . . . 67

Chapter 7 – Physical Evolution:
My Body Is a Sacred Temple . . . . . . . . . . . . . . 79

Chapter 8 – Social Evolution:
My World Is Our World and Welcome to It . . . . . . 85

Chapter 9 – Childhood Evolution:
It's Never Too Late to Recapture My Heart
and Have a Happy Childhood . . . . . . . . . . . . . 93

Appendix:
Actions for Moving from Limiting Beliefs
to Evolving/Empowering Beliefs . . . . . . . . . . . .103

{ CHAPTER 1 }

# PERSONAL EVOLUTION:
## The Never-Ending Journey toward the Possible You

EVOLUTION IS RELENTLESS. Physical evolution from walking on all fours to walking erect took thousands of years. Meanwhile, consciousness and intelligence have also been evolving.

Personal evolution is unique for each individual. It is a lifetime of climbing an infinite mountain. There are places where you take a break. But the higher you go the better you feel. The top of the mountain is perfection, and no human being gets there (at least none that I have ever known).

Personal evolution is suppressed by Limiting Beliefs (LBs) such as "I'm not very smart, attractive, or lovable." They create the fears that lead to feeling weak, being defensive, and attempting to control others and life in general.

Nobody begins life with Limiting Beliefs. But self-doubts begin early and are reinforced by other people and situations. Limiting Beliefs inhibit the real, the successful, the loving, the lovable you—the you that is beyond belief.

Evolving/Empowering Beliefs (EBs) move you toward greater self-love and the ability to give and receive love. They create the profound, transformative changes that leave you feeling best about yourself—alive, powerful, and in control.

The good news is that it doesn't make any difference where you are at any moment of your personal evolution. Every day is just the starting point for developing more of your limitless capacity to evolve spiritually, emotionally, sexually, intellectually, creatively, physically, socially, and in your career.

This book, for the most part, contains stories from my eighty-plus years of moving beyond Limiting Beliefs to Evolving/Empowering Beliefs. I tell my journey because, rather than instructing others on what to do or how they should be, I think sharing ourselves is the most effective way of empowering others.

The book is relevant for both men and women because most of the beliefs that limit personal evolution are held in common. Plus, in the appendix are exercises for your personal evolution, including how to turn Limiting Beliefs into Evolving/Empowering Beliefs.

> **LB:** *Masculinity and femininity are defined by traits.*
> **EB:** *My true identity is my heart and soul.*

Early in life, the awareness that we are unique beings sets us off on a quest to establish our own identity. I don't remember when I had that awareness. I do know that reconciling my feelings and behavior with what conventional thinking defined as gender traits has been a major part of my evolutionary struggle.

Until my first day at a new school in a new town, I had never thought much about being masculine. My first nine years growing up in Philadelphia were nondescript. What little I remember include taking long walks with my grandfather in the park, the Japanese attack on Pearl Harbor, and playing jump rope at school. I never played sports or went to sporting events, and television hadn't even been invented. And then we moved to Los Angeles.

In preparation for the beginning of the new semester, my mother took me shopping for new slacks, dress shirts, and shoes. I arrived at school a painfully shy kid dressed like little Lord Fauntleroy and just wanting to blend in. As the only boy not dressed in jeans, tee shirt, and tennis shoes, that plan quickly went awry.

To my great chagrin, during recess, the girls formed a circle around me and danced some kind of welcome ceremony. But the worst part was when the boys chose sides to play either kickball or tetherball. Not knowing the difference between a kickball and a tetherball, I huddled next to a brick building, lost and confused.

Returning home in tears, my mother and I hustled off to the nearest clothing store to outfit me in the proper uniform. My perfect slacks and shirts hung neatly in the closet until I outgrew them.

I decided that to be like the other boys I needed to make myself into an athlete. That began years of honing my skills while studiously learning the techniques and rules of every major sport. In my quest to become "a guy," I made myself into a competitive athlete.

It wasn't long before I discovered that those skills were not helpful in the next masculine endeavor, girls and sex. The new contest became pursuing girls with the dedication of an athlete. I became a sex-obsessed, macho, competitive sexual athlete.

My most manly accomplishment occurred in my twenties when I snared the trophy blond former cheerleader. However, it didn't take long for my world to crack. This beautiful shapely body turned out to also have a brilliant inquisitive mind that challenged everything I had learned about being a man.

Unless you are of my generation, you may not know what it was like in 1963 to be with a woman who wanted me to share my feelings, not tell jokes that demeaned women, be concerned for her sexual pleasure, and be sensitive to her feelings. It was like asking a man to know what it feels like to go through childbirth. Real men weren't interested in those things, were they?

Enter the men's liberation movement and my next foray into trying to be a man. Alas, after many workshops beating drums, listening to poetry, shouting out my anger, and finding my warrior, I was still no closer to feeling secure within myself. In fact, I was being led away from my essence by ideas from well-meaning leaders of the men's movement.

After fifty-three years of pretzeling (don't bother looking it up) myself into the man I was supposed to be, I was still driven to pursue masculine qualities such as control, winning, and being right. I didn't have a clue as to what it meant to be so comfortable with all parts of myself that I didn't have to prove anything. And I certainly didn't feel comfortable embracing my feminine, whatever the hell that was.

My world was rocked with the ending of my twenty-six-year marriage, retiring from a successful and fulfilling career, leaving the house I loved, and moving from the town I had lived in for forty-five years to a small town in the Rocky Mountains.

It was here, with the support of an evolved male best friend, wonderful people, and books from various self-help and spiritual disciplines and vigorously working my 12-Step Co-dependence Anonymous program, that I engaged in a discovery process that led to the rebirth of parts of myself that had been buried for a very long time.

The most important lesson I've learned is that my true identity is my heart. I use the heart as a metaphor for the part of me that embodies my essence. (I see soul, higher self, spirit, or true nature as interchangeable with heart). I know that only when I'm connected to my heart, can I connect in satisfying ways to others and to the mystery that lies beyond humanness.

When I think of the times that I feel best about myself, they all accompany my heart being open. I remember the:

- ecstasy of falling in love,
- freedom of dancing with abandon,
- rapture while listening to music,
- connection of being touched emotionally while watching a film,
- magnificence of watching a sunset,
- fulfillment of playing on the floor with my eight-month-old granddaughter,
- spirituality of seeing deeply into the soul of my partner while making love,
- pride of giving my support to a person in need,
- satisfaction of engaging in a meaningful conversation.

Those times feel like coming home. They are magical. In addition to knowing that home is where my heart is, I know that heart is where my home is.

I like to use the analogy of skiing in the zone to remind me of what it means to be in my heart. The zone is a peak experience. It is being centered and in the moment. Basketball players describe it as time slowing down and the basket seeming to be much larger in diameter. The zone has been described in the titles of the best-selling books of Mihaly Csikszentmihalyi as *Flow* and Eckhart Tolle as *The Power of Now*.

In the zone, my skiing is effortless and graceful. I am perfectly balanced, and I feel connected to everything around me. When I lose that connection, I go off-center. Skiing out of balance is not wrong. It just takes more effort, and it is not as beautiful and graceful. Although skiing out of the zone can be enjoyable, it does not come close to the perfection and the high of skiing in the zone.

When I realized the ecstasy of skiing in a centered place, I became dedicated to skiing more of the time from that incredible place. That required recognizing when I was not centered, discovering how to get back to center, and learning how to stay there more of the time. That is the exact process I use in my everyday life.

Living with a Limiting Belief is like skiing off center. I'm not bad or wrong for having the belief. It just keeps me out of balance and from finding the fulfillment that comes from living congruently with my essence.

A good example of a Limiting Belief is defining masculinity by traits or characteristics. Because there is no room for feminine characteristics, it is unbalanced and, yes, limiting.

On the other hand, believing that my true identity is my heart is freeing and limitless. When my heart guides me, I have faith, a sense of meaning, and self-esteem. I am fully present in the moment and, most importantly, open to learning. (Much more about what it means to be heart connected is in chapter 2, "Emotional Evolution.")

Shedding Limiting Beliefs is like physical growth. While growing up, it's hard to recognize how much growth occurs each day. Seeing the difference in size between an infant and the finished product is amazing. Similarly, the changes from shedding Limiting Beliefs may not be apparent in the moment, but comparing what I was years ago to what I am now is amazing.

It's like peeling an infinite artichoke. Each leaf has a Limiting Belief on one side, the sweet meat of an Evolving/Empowering Belief on the other, and a thorn. To enjoy the sweetness, I must avoid the thorn. But the real prize is that the more leaves I peel, the more available becomes my heart.

Knowing that masculinity cannot be defined by traits and I no longer have to prove that I'm a man feels great. I think we are all better served by being rid of that limiting term (of course, that goes for femininity as well). In fact, I would go even further and posit that we are better off not defining any group by traits.

Rumi, the thirteenth century Persian poet, Islamic scholar, and Sufi mystic wrote, "Beyond right doing and wrong doing there is another field. I'll meet you there."

To paraphrase Rumi: Beyond masculine, feminine, American, Asian, Jew, Christian, black, white, conservative, liberal, and so on, there is another field. I'll meet you there.

{ Chapter 2 }

# Emotional Evolution:
## I'm Full of It and I Love It

WE STOPPED ALONG THE ROAD TO SEE THE SUNSET.
"Wow, that's beautiful!" she said breathlessly.
"Yeah, it's really nice," I intoned.
"Look at all those colors and the patterns. Isn't it fantastic?" she said.
"It's pretty."
"How can you be so unresponsive?"
Annoyed I answered, "What do you want me to do, dance?"
"Why not? You know, the only time I see you expressing real enthusiasm and excitement is when you're watching a sporting event. I'd like some of that excitement in response to me and the things we do together."

Letting go at a sporting event was allowable behavior but in other situations was risky. If someone thought my emotion was inappropriate, I might hear, "That's a dumb way to feel," "You're immature," "What a sissy," or "You're weak."

Scared, scared, scared. Feelings were unacceptable, except at important events like sporting events and funerals. Keeping my responses controlled at a low level was sure a lot safer than reacting spontaneously and risking criticism.

Heartfelt feelings are the scariest things in the world. If you don't think so, just consider the comment I heard during a therapy session. He was an ex-Marine helicopter pilot who had served two years in Vietnam. She was on the verge of divorcing him because she felt so disconnected and lonely in their relationship.

"All I want," she said, "is to know you. Why won't you share your feelings with me?"

He thought for a moment and then this American hero who was willing to face death everyday he flew his helicopter into battle looked at the floor and said in a whisper, "It's too dangerous."

> **LB:** *All feelings are the same.*
> **EB:** *Knowing the difference between heartfelt and protected feelings is essential for my well-being.*

Feelings are what make us unique. Like fluctuations on a life-support monitor, they reflect the highs and lows of life as they animate both ecstasy and pain. Contrast this to the flat line signifying the end of life. This accurately describes the victims of acculturation who died a long time ago and are just waiting for the actual event to take place.

For years, New Thought gurus exhorted me to express my feelings. I went to workshops to learn how to express my feelings. Some focused particularly on anger, and I became pretty good at expressing my anger.

One day, my partner and I were having an argument. She was sitting in our big overstuffed chair, and I was standing over her. We were going back and forth in one of our typical battles yelling and screaming at each other. She could give and take with the best of them.

But something happened that had never happened before. After a few minutes she stopped yelling, curled up in a ball and began sobbing. Through her tears she said, "I feel awful, and it feels like I'm about to die."

"Aw, come on," I chided her, "you've never said that before. I've yelled at you lots of times, and you always just yell back or get up and stomp out."

"Yeah, but I think I always feel this way. I've never wanted to let you see it. I probably never even wanted myself to know it. But I think that under my anger and defensiveness there's always this pain."

I immediately softened, and we began the first of many discussions about feelings.

I came to understand protective anger as a secondary emotion covering pain and sadness. The human brain, which has the incredible ability to think abstractly and create wondrous ideas, also creates the protective feelings that cover heartfelt feelings. The following is what I have learned about the difference between heartfelt and protected feelings.

Although the ability to feel is natural, feelings do not always come from an open heart. Heartfelt feelings are warm, tender, sensual, and caring. However, their expression in tears, laughter, and compassion leave me vulnerable to the sting of criticism from others, as well as from myself.

Cold, harsh, and uncaring feelings such as blame, arrogance, disdain, and jealousy are protective. They cover more vulnerable heartfelt feelings and reflect a disconnection from my heart. Even sadness and pain when coming from a "poor me" victim place are not heartfelt.

Heartfelt feelings are my authentic self, my essence, my soul. When I embrace them, they find their natural expressions fully and passionately. Laughter is not stuck in my throat, and sadness is not repressed behind my eyes. Each expression becomes a childlike (not childish) outpouring that consumes my entire body while both bathing and cleansing me. I am full of it, and I love it!

The free expression of heartfelt feelings opens to simultaneously giving and receiving love. It forges a heartfelt engagement with myself and unlocks the door to deep and meaningful connections with others.

For heartfelt feelings to be nurtured and protected feelings to be learned from, it is essential to know the difference between heartfelt and protected feelings. A more complete list of heartfelt and protective feelings can be found in the appendix. The heartfelt feelings that encompass most others are discussed below.

## Sadness and Tears

I have always been a very sensitive person. In my youth, I often tried to hold back my tears. I sometimes wanted to cry during movies, but by clenching my face or deflecting my thoughts, I fought back the tears.

Most of the time I was successful, but I would walk out of the theater with a pounding at the back of my neck and a head that felt twice its size. If I was with another person, I held myself together by walking briskly and avoiding eye contact or conversation.

Embracing this exquisitely sensitive part of myself, and moving easily into tears, has been a gradual process. In addition to expressing pain, my tears often accompany joy and awe. I love experiences that touch me deeply. For example, there are some films that I watch over and over again; I love the experience that the tears evoke.

I am proud that I can be touched emotionally and am not afraid to show that part of myself. When I'm with a person whom I care deeply about, we hold each other, experiencing together the comfort and delicious intimacy of a shared heartfelt connection. Giving myself permission to express my authentic self leaves me feeling proud and powerful.

## Joy and Laughter

The Jesuit mystic and archeologist Pierre Teilhard de Chardin said, "Joy is the sign of the presence of God." When I am not self-conscious and worried about being judged, I just flow, and life is fun. Joy expresses the love in what I'm doing.

To see the silver lining and play with the capriciousness of life, rather than getting bogged down, requires seeing the lighter side of things. It means living as the Buddhist saying advises, "Act always as if the future of the Universe depends on what you do, while laughing at yourself for thinking that whatever you do makes any difference."

Feeling joy requires not taking things so seriously. One time, I thought back to the countless number of times I became upset with something like being late, a spilled glass of milk, a disappointment, or how I looked physically. Then I thought, *Why did I make such a big deal over that? It doesn't seem very important right now. What if life is not intended to be such a serious affair?*

Laughter is the natural expression of joy. I never knew the difference between a ha-ha laugh emanating from a constricted throat and a belly laugh that consumed my entire body . . . until I smoked marijuana for the first time. I got high with a friend, and we went back and forth with the silliest quips that left me rolling on the floor in laughter. I laughed until my stomach hurt.

Later on as we talked about our experience, she said, "I've never seen you that way."

I responded, "I've never been that way."

Unleashing the genie of laughter was an unforgettable experience that left me spent and satisfied. I knew I wanted more, but I also knew I did not want to become dependent on anything outside myself for that experience. So began a journey to discover and resolve the fears that left me unable to feel and express the fullness of joy.

## Compassion and Empathy

Compassion is feeling empathy toward others and myself in all feeling states, not just in suffering. It produces the feelings and behavior that create openhearted engagement with others and is the gateway to my spirituality.

With heartfelt compassion, the sacred within me is illuminated, and it is impossible to run roughshod over the sacred that lies within others. At those times:

- play cannot be a win/lose contest;
- touch cannot be inappropriately sexual or harmful;
- productivity cannot mistreat others or the environment;
- feelings cannot be criticized or repressed; and
- learning cannot be blocked.

## Forgiveness

Forgiveness as a natural extension of compassion differs significantly from traditional ideas about forgiveness. Traditional concepts of forgiveness, which can occur without compassion, allow behavior to be categorized into right and wrong boxes. That kind of forgiveness is merely a pardoning of transgressions. Waving the wand of absolution is condescending and alienating and locks the forgiver into feelings of self-righteousness and blame.

Holding a grudge or being defensive and angry binds me to those feelings and judgments. Alienated from heartfelt feelings, I cannot forgive myself, and therefore, I can neither receive forgiveness nor forgive others. Traditional forgiveness does not help overcome this alienation and is therefore not nurturing to others or myself.

Compassionate forgiveness, however, understands that, given my fears and ignorance, both others and I are always doing the best we can. We are neither wrong nor bad. In reality, there is nothing to forgive; there is only acceptance.

Acceptance of situations and behaviors follows from compassion. Feeling deeply into a situation averts any critical judgment or a desire to change anything. I naturally accept that people and situations are exactly as they must be. Whenever compassionate acceptance is lost, learning the very important reasons that situations are as they are reconnects me to heartfelt feelings and to acceptance.

Acceptance does not condone behavior. It does not mean that some actions are not harmful; I still need to protect myself from predators. It does not take away my sadness over what I missed due to my own fears and disconnected behaviors or the fear or behavior of others.

When I am truly accepting, I know that things in the past could not have been any different, and forgiveness follows naturally. Acceptance allows me to forgive myself, and that is where true healing begins.

Compassionate forgiveness enables me to feel better about myself and have more experiences that leave me feeling really powerful. An exercise to practice compassionate forgiveness can be found in the appendix.

## Faith

Faith lies in knowing that, no matter what life gives me, I will survive. Faith is the opposite of control. I know I cannot have control over the future, and I do not have to know the future because it does not matter.

The more I realize that I can survive anything, including failures, abandonment, betrayal, disasters, and even death, the more faith I have. Then I have less need for control over the future actions of people and events.

A deeper level of faith requires more than just knowing I will survive. It means believing in my ability to thrive—to pick myself up, learn from the experience, and emerge better off than I was before. It is the faith that connection to my heart will result in the behavior that leads to getting what I truly desire.

When fear gives way to faith, I can allow room for both others and myself to be our unique selves. As faith grows, my ability to let go of control and live in harmony with life increases. By not having my behavior dictated by fear, I feel more powerful and I thrive.

> **LB:** *I am inadequate and unlovable, and when other people are upset, I am responsible for their unhappiness; and when I am upset with other people, they are responsible for my unhappiness.*
> **EB:** *I am not responsible for how other people react to something I have done; and others are not to blame for my unhappiness or upsets.*

I do not believe I came into this world believing that I was unlovable and responsible for the upsets of others. I adopted these beliefs in childhood as a result of taking the actions of other people personally.

For the most part, my self-doubts began when adults got upset over things I did. I may have been doing natural things like crying or exploring my body and other parts of my environment. Adults may have gotten angry, made derisive comments, or just gotten cold and withdrawn their love; but the message was clear—my actions were wrong, and I was responsible for their upsets.

As a child, I had no way of knowing that in another home, culture, or era, my behavior might not be judged as wrong. In my innocence, I formed the belief that when others are upset with me, I am wrong and responsible for their upset and should do something to make them feel better.

Once I believed I was responsible for another person's upset, it followed that the other was responsible and to blame when I was upset and should do something to make me feel better. Blaming others for my feelings became one of my favorite pastimes. I would self-righteously think or yell: "You make me sick" or "You're really upsetting me."

The conventional thinking that caused me to blame others stemmed from the belief that forces outside me were responsible for my unhappiness. So when I was unhappy, it was the fault of my spouse, God, circumstances, or yes, even my children.

Guilt thrived on these two Limiting Beliefs. They were attempts, usually unconscious, to manipulate others and avoid taking responsibility for my feelings and my life.

Escaping from carrying these beliefs into adulthood is almost impossible. For that to happen, I would have either experienced someone taking responsibility for his or her feelings or possessed the wisdom to not take personally the critical judgments of others. For the former to occur, someone would have reacted to being upset by taking responsibility for his or her feelings with an intention to learn. He or she would have been curious. This contemplative attitude would have been reflected in questions like:

- "I wonder why I'm getting so upset?"
- "What are my fears and beliefs that are getting touched off right now?"
- "What's going on with you and why are you behaving as you are?" or
- "What can I learn from this upset?

I do not remember any of those responses ever happening.

As a child, to not take the judgments of others personally, I would have had to look up into the eyes of an important person who was upset and think, *It's not that I'm unlovable; it's that you're having trouble loving me right now.* That was always the truth, but since a child cannot be expected to know that, I learned to take the upsets of others personally.

Eventually I came to know that I am not and never was bad, inadequate, or unlovable. Unloving responses come from a closed heart, and I am never responsible for the fears that cause people to close their hearts.

On the other hand, when I blame any outside force for how I am feeling about any of my experiences in life, I literally give away all my power.

> **LB:** *My happiness and sense of well-being come from things outside myself.*
> **EB:** *I am capable of creating my sense of well-being.*

As a child, I was dependent on others for my well-being, literally for my survival. Maturity requires growing out of neediness into the independence that opens the door to interdependence. Unfortunately, almost everything in my life worked to perpetuate dependence.

My parents were too frightened to allow me to explore and develop independence. Instead, I was constantly told how to think, feel, and behave and punished for not living up to their standards.

Often well-meaning caregivers, relatives, and school and religious teachers did not assist me in learning how to go inside and discover my inner resources for well-being. When experiencing loss or failure, instead of someone swooping in to try to make it better, I was never assisted in learning to nurture myself.

Thus began a dependency on others to tell me what to do and how to feel. This dependency also transferred to things outside me, such as television, food, sex, relationships, and work.

A dependency existed around anything I believed I needed for my sense of well-being. I feared losing or not having my desired object. When I was without it, I felt lost and out of sorts. I obsessively thought about and craved my drug of choice.

I even believed that I loved it. But in any dependency, in whatever patterns that were developed, there was one constant—I secretly resented anything upon which I was dependent. The alcoholic does not love alcohol any more than the compulsive eater really loves food.

To stay in my heart and fully love something or someone, I must be free of dependency. My involvement, whether that be with a substance or a person, is then out of choice not fear.

> **LB:** *I need other people to tell me how I should feel and what I should do.*
> **EB:** *The answers to my life's journey reside within me and sometimes I need others to help access these answers.*

After telling my therapist that my wife had decided to end our relationship, I sat back and sighed, "What do you think I should do?"

She responded sympathetically, "I wish I could give you some simple ideas that would make your pain immediately disappear, but I can't. I take back what I just said; even if I could wave a magic wand, I wouldn't. I don't believe that either protecting you from your pain or giving you advice is what you need.

"I want to help you discover how to trust your inner knowing. That will be truly empowering. When connected to your essence, what you should do will become clear, and the results will be satisfying. Until that time, we can explore what's creating your unhappiness. I'll suggest some reading material that will help you."

Over the next few months, I worked diligently on myself. I read, talked with friends, and came into each therapy session ready with feelings and issues I wanted to learn more about.

> **LB:** *I cannot handle disappointment, failure, or rejection, and I am wrong and bad when I make mistakes.*
> **EB:** *Disappointment, failure, mistakes, and rejection are opportunities to learn and evolve.*

I spent a great deal of my life in a self-imposed prison. I was willing to sacrifice my happiness in the present to protect myself from any future potential unhappiness. I believed I was fragile, that I couldn't take it if I were hurt emotionally. I was never sure what "take it," meant but I sure didn't want to find out. When I finally confronted this Limiting Belief, I discovered that I had in fact withstood a great deal of emotional pain.

In my past relationships, I had often been rejected. But as devastated as I felt during those times, I survived. I had been terribly disappointed in others and myself. Still, I had bounced back. In reality, I didn't fall apart.

Today when I allow myself to react to things around me, my feelings are intensified. If I'm flying high and something brings me down, the crash may be painful, humiliating, and depressing. I don't want to feel those lows. But I need to remember that when I get hurt, I can survive the pain.

Taking responsibility means not blaming myself. I try to remember that, given my Limiting Beliefs and fears at any particular point in time, I am always doing the best I possibly can. Learning a new way of thinking is the process of moving beyond my Limiting Beliefs. It takes time, and I must be patient with myself.

> **LB:** *I need to be in a primary relationship with a woman.*
> **EB:** *I can create my well-being whether I am in or out of a relationship.*

One morning as we talked about how love was all tied up with need, I blurted out, "But if I didn't need you, why would I be with you?"

"Because we like being together and we offer each other some wonderful things," she answered.

Sometime later, I realized that the desperate energy of need is the antithesis of love. Yet with song lyrics such as, "I can't live if living is without you," my culture had taught me the romantic love of neediness.

That was the beginning of confronting one of my deepest beliefs—I couldn't make myself happy. I had depended on women to take care of me emotionally, just as a child depends on a parent.

To the outside world, I'm sure I didn't look needy. I was successful and self-assured in both my professional and social activities. But at home, I was a needy child depending on Mommy to make me happy. Of course, I could entertain myself with reading, television, or work, but I was always secretly waiting for the time she and I would spend together.

Although I was convinced that without a woman I could not be happy or successful, I also knew from years of learning about relationships that I had to deal with my dependency issues. I knew that since the world was full of women who were conditioned to be caretakers that I could probably find one.

When my marriage ended, to confront my biggest demons, I decided to go cold turkey. I made a commitment to not be in an intimate relationship until I felt comfortable that I was no longer a relationship and sexual addict (more about my sexual addiction in the next chapter).

What did it mean to be able to be happy on my own and to find joy in anything I was doing? I had never considered that before. It would mean that I would be happy both when I was in a relationship and when I was not.

There were not many things I did in which I found joy, and I knew I had to find more of them. But the deeper issue was how to find joy in *whatever* I was doing.

Over the years, I have grown to feel confident that I can create my own sense of well-being and do not need a woman to do that for me. It feels great being freed from the fear of being alone.

I would never suggest that the extreme measure I took is the only way to break such an addiction, but it worked for me. Today, I feel reasonably sure that I will not compromise my integrity out of fear of losing a relationship. I feel reasonably sure that I will not withdraw my love when my partner explores and pursues her needs. I feel reasonably sure that I will stay centered, even when my partner loses her center and even if that means she criticizes or blames me.

All these things I feel reasonably sure I will discover with certainty only when they are tested in an intimate relationship.

> **LB:** *In the face of difficulties, others need to change for things to be okay.*
> **EB:** *In any difficulty, all participants share responsibility, and there are no victims.*

Getting intractably stuck in the righteousness of a position is a sure-fire recipe for endless upsets, arguments, and emotional distance. Believing others are primarily responsible for the problems in my relationships and if only they would change then everything would be all right leaves me as a powerless victim.

Trying to get others to change their thinking and behavior and their resisting those attempts inevitably lead to power struggles. Power struggles can exist in any relationship. Between committed adults, they run the gamut of beliefs and desires from things such as religion, politics, and sex to seemingly mundane things such as overneatness, timeliness, and eating habits. Between parents and children, power struggles can be about homework, manners, messiness, or language. Between religions and political parties, they crop up around the right way to think and act.

A power struggle is analogous to one person standing on a pier throwing out a line with a hook on the end that a person in the water bites onto. As they struggle, the one with the hook in her mouth shouts, "You know, if you hadn't thrown out this hook, we wouldn't be having this struggle!"

The one who has thrown out the hook snaps back, "Oh yeah? Well, if you hadn't bitten onto the hook, we wouldn't be in this mess!"

As long as the one who has bitten blames the one who threw and tries to get him to stop throwing out hooks, and the one who has thrown blames the one who has bitten and tries to get her to stop biting onto hooks, while they both get to be self-righteous, they are stuck.

It doesn't matter who started the fracas. Each one has a part in the problem. She assumes personal power when she opens to learning about why she keeps biting onto hooks (her buttons). He assumes personal power by learning about why he keeps throwing out hooks (pushing her buttons).

It takes only one of them to change for their entire system to change. When he resolves his need to bait her, there is no problem. Or alternatively, if he keeps throwing out the bait and she no longer bites, there will be no struggle. Acknowledging that relationship difficulties are part of a system to which we each contribute throws off the yoke of the victim.

The idea of equal responsibility for problems that result from conflict is unpopular not only with marriage partners. It is eschewed by parents in difficulties with children, by bosses in difficulties with employees, and most definitely, by nations in their difficulties with other nations.

> **LB:** *Conflicts end with winners and loser so must be either won or avoided.*
> **EB:** *Engaging in conflicts with open hearts is an opportunity to evolve and grow closer.*

Conflict! To this day, the mere mention of the word sends shudders through my body. In an oyster, two opposing elements being rubbed together produce something of beauty that is prized. In human beings, seemingly incompatible elements being rubbed together usually produce nothing but a waste product.

My tendency to be conflict phobic is certainly understandable. I grew up with a mother and father who withdrew from conflict by never confronting anything. Meanwhile, my mother and sister constantly fought with threats and harsh words.

My mother's often-heard complaints were that she was the miserable victim of a withdrawn and unavailable husband or her ungrateful, selfish daughter. I became a scarred (and scared) little boy escaping as much as possible to the playground or the homes of friends.

I learned that in an upset there were only two alternatives, fighting or withdrawal. The only two outcomes were winners or losers. Conflict became inextricably entwined with loss, pain, crying, yelling, being hurt, being scared, being in the middle, being responsible for another's unhappiness. No matter how big I grew, the little boy with an omnipresent fear of conflict responded by either avoiding it or engaging with the consciousness of a warrior.

These ideas about conflict not only were demonstrated in my home; they also were in evidence all around me. My boyhood movie and television heroes were combatants using power to win and be right. Conflicts were "do or die" battles. Whether on the battlefield or in the Wild West, courtroom dramas or family situations, the mighty won, and the vanquished slunk off in humiliation.

I learned to engage only when I thought I had the power to win or when things became so bad that I was willing to risk loss. Therefore, when upset, I would typically disengage until either reaching a breaking point or feeling strong enough to engage.

Engagement meant steeling myself while aggressively using my words to convince the other that I was right. In withdrawal, I would quietly agree but inside feel angry and resentful.

Withdrawal is by far my most common response to upsets. Nonetheless, shutting down and withdrawing into indifference, rather than standing up for something that is important, not only disrespects myself but, because it withholds the truth, is disrespectful to the other.

It is no wonder why anytime my partner was disappointed or said, "Something's really upsetting me, and we really need to talk," I felt an immediate tension.

One particular battle that led to a breakthrough in my thinking about conflict remains emblazoned in my mind. During this bout, she and I were verbally bobbing and weaving around a free-standing cutting board in our kitchen. Suddenly she stopped the usual sparring over the issue (I have no idea what the issue was) and said softly and with concern, "You seem scared. What are you feeling?"

Not expecting that, I was pulled up short. My immediate response was, "What are you talking about? I'm not scared; I'm mad."

Not to be dissuaded, she continued, "I often feel during our disagreements like we're in a life-or-death struggle. I think I steel myself when I get scared, and that feels awful. But right now, I'm sense your fear."

Disarmed, I dropped my guard, and as some of the fear drained from my body, I became aware of how differently I felt. "I guess I do get scared, but it's not of some physical confrontation." We both laughed at my feeble attempt at some humor. After all, I was six feet tall, and she was a five-foot-two-inch midget.

"You know," I mused, "I never thought of it before, but when we're in an argument, I feel like I'm two years old and you're my looming mother." Childhood memories and fears flooded, and we talked about our fears and reactions that got each of us locked into battles instead of open discussions.

The goal to learn from a conflict and gain clarity, rather than to win or be right, is a complete shift of energy. I feel it in my body. In an interaction where there is an intention to win, I feel tense and tight. I may feel the rush of excitement that accompanies a battle, and I may feel good if I win and bad if I lose.

With an intention to learn, there is far less tension. There is excitement, but it is the kind generated by the aha of discovery. Discussion on these terms sets the tone to either continue and deepen that particular exploration or begin explorations in new and uncharted waters. There are only winners.

Whenever I am open to learning, I'm connected to my heart. Whenever I'm in a battle or withdrawn, I have lost my heart connection. Choosing a different path begins with the awareness that I'm in a protective interaction.

Once I'm connected to my heart, I can make amends and heal any wounds that accompanied my protectiveness. Expressing my sadness about any wounding that occurred when I was protected might be as simple statement as, "I realize that I got thrown off by what you did. My irritation was disrespectful, and I feel badly about that."

Making amends and healing wounds is the crucial step that is almost never taken after a protective interaction. It is not protective interactions that lead to serious relationship problems. Serious problems fester and grow when protective behaviors persist and are not cleaned up. An exercise for disengaging and recentering can be found in the appendix.

In most cases, the lack of a heartfelt response is not because I intended to be disrespectful. I was probably unaware of the effects my behavior was having on others, just as I had gotten used to absorbing disrespectful behavior directed toward me.

In the heat of the moment, like most people, I would lose my heart connection. An important step in maintaining that connection more of the time is becoming more accepting of myself when I disconnect from my heart. Remembering in those moments that I'm not bad or wrong, just insecure, really helps.

As I recover my innate excitement for learning, instead of viewing this self-discovery journey as a burdensome task, it has become enjoyable!

> **LB:** *Emotional intimacy is just a romantic dream.*
> **EB:** *Emotional intimacy can be continually nurtured.*

Emotional intimacy happens when open hearts meet. It satisfies my deep and rarely met need to be seen, understood, valued, and appreciated. Tasting the experience of being unguarded and vulnerable together is a delicious connection.

We are giving of ourselves without any attachment to getting something in return. Whatever we are doing, whether moving in sync to the same rhythm, sharing tears, laughing together uncontrollably, playing uninhibitedly, making love, or talking from the heart, we are simply flowing in the moment.

The quality of my experiences stand in stark contrast when I compare the conversations that were dominated by fun, caring, and listening with those focused on making a point or showing off intellectual expertise.

For example, I contrast the times when I played a game that was just for fun with those events when competition and winning were the focus. And I recall sexual experiences distinguished by sharing and caring and those that were self-centered.

Emotional intimacy requires each partner's freedom to express his or her deepest feelings and fulfill his or her heartfelt desires. Two hearts beating as one must remain two hearts. The heart of intimacy will not allow anyone's needs to be compromised. The openness of compassion and learning will not rest until relationship and individuality exist simultaneously.

> **LB:** *Since women are more emotional than men, it is not manly for a man to be emotional.*
> **EB:** *Men are as emotional as women, and feeling and expressing feelings are integral parts of being a person.*

Realizing that everything that makes me truly happy happens naturally when I am connected to my heart has taken me on the ride of my life. It has meant uncovering a part of myself that had been buried for a very long time. It feels so good to embrace such an integral part of my being. Thinking of that beautiful little boy forced to bite his lip so as not to cry brings me to tears right now.

When I'm connected to my heart, I cannot compromise my integrity, nor will I compromise the integrity of another person. My true power lies in my ability to feel things deeply *and* not lose my way. It has taken a lot of personal work, but I am learning to trust my heart.

I'm gaining more confidence in my heart being both soft *and* strong. When I'm connected to it, I both feel compassion with others and am not defenseless. My heart will not allow me to compromise my integrity.

When my heart guides me, I have the strength of Gandhi, Alice Stokes Paul, and Martin Luther King who when confronted with hostile enemies said no without resorting to violence. I have the strength of the aikido master who, when attacked, skillfully and without anger or malice leads his opponent to the ground.

I am proud that I can be touched emotionally and am not afraid to show that part. My willingness to courageously let my heartfelt emotions guide me makes me stronger than hiding my true feelings out of fear of rejection or ridicule. After all, who are stronger, those who feel deeply but hold back out of fear or those who authentically show what they are feeling?

Of the myriad beliefs that limited my freedom to feel and my ability to live life fully and show up authentically, two fascinate me because they have been so pervasive for so long: (1) women are more emotional than men and (2) men are more sexual than women.

I know that I am as emotional as any woman, in fact, as most women I encounter. I believe that if men had not been repressing their feelings since childhood they would be as emotional as women, and maybe even more so. I hope this chapter helps send belief #1 into the dustbin of history.

If women were not taught to repress their sexuality, would they be more sexual than men? Stay tuned. The next chapter begins that discussion.

{ CHAPTER 3 }

# SEXUAL EVOLUTION:
## Keeping My Heart On

In a 1970s film, the name of which I can't remember, the lead actress tells her mother that she's in therapy because she can't have an orgasm. The mother gives her a disapproving look and says, "Well, we didn't have those in my day." (It might have been *Lovers and Other Strangers*.)

Well, those were my days. Growing up, sex was never mentioned in my house. There were no popular magazines that showed a woman's body. I was a sexually frustrated and obsessed teenager and young adult.

My first sexual relationships were awful. I was as clueless as my partners. I knew nothing about a woman's sexuality, her needs, her clitoris, or her orgasm. In fact, I don't think I had ever been with a woman who had had an orgasm.

I didn't begin evolving sexually until I was almost thirty and in my first relationship with a woman who wanted to discuss and learn about sex. Our openness to learning about each other and ourselves was one of the things that brought us close together.

With a lot of talking and understanding, she had her first. As time went on, her orgasms grew more intense, and she started having multiple orgasms. In all my relationships, I had always been the aggressor and wanted sex more than my partner. She was becoming very sexual, and I was a little uneasy.

> **LB:** *Men are more sexual than women, and if a woman is more sexual than me, I am less of a man.*
> **EB:** *Her sexuality does not diminish my manliness, and I am in awe of her sexual capacity.*

Conventional wisdom taught me that men were more sexual than women. It naturally followed that I would be the aggressor and want sex more often than she did.

I would say things like, "I want you to be more sexual," "I enjoy you being turned on," and "I love experiencing your orgasm." But something held me back from fully participating in her becoming more sexually responsive.

Eventually, I got in touch with some of my fears about her sexual capacity. If she became more sexual and her increased sexual capacity dwarfed mine, would that diminish my sense of masculinity? What if she wanted sex and I wasn't up for her needs? Could I satisfy her? Would she leave me for a better lover?

To fully support and celebrate her sexuality, I had to come to terms with some basic facts such as:

- Since she did not have to have an erection to engage in sexual activity, she could participate in sexual activity more easily and for longer periods.
- After orgasm, I would have to wait for a time before being able to have another; she could not only continue but also have multiple orgasms.
- She was capable of more intense and longer-lasting orgasms.

The more I resolved my Limiting Beliefs about sexuality, the more I was able to fully participate in her sexuality. I became more comfortable in:

- giving up control and allowing her to direct the experience (this is similar to becoming the follower rather than the leader while ballroom dancing, which can be a wonderful learning experience);
- lying back and, without doing anything to her, allowing her to give me pleasure;
- appreciating the intensity of her response;
- allowing her to direct me into giving her what she wanted and needed, rather than what I thought she wanted and needed;
- slowing down.

Isn't it something after all these millennia of trying to force ourselves into the boxes that men are more sexual than women and women are more emotional than men that these deeply engrained beliefs are false?!

Primitive man must have created these myths because they so feared their own highly sensitive nature and the sexual power of women (let alone other female powers). Given the conditions that existed when they were created, these beliefs are understandable.

But what purpose does it serve to perpetuate them today? And how many more patently false beliefs running our lives are there? And what revolutionary changes would occur were we to live in integrity with who we really are? Just asking.

> **LB:** *I should be ready, willing, and able whenever she is.*
> **EB:** *When my sexuality is connected to my emotions, I may not always feel like having sex.*

A woman once said to me, "I need an emotional connection to fire my sexuality. When we're not connected emotionally, my sexuality goes out the window." I thought that was one of the nuttiest things I had ever heard, and I told her so in no uncertain terms.

In addition to searching outside the window for her sexuality, I spent time explaining why there was something wrong with her. I told her I didn't need to feel emotionally connected (whatever that meant) to feel sexual. I told her that I felt sexual when I woke up in the morning, at night when we got into bed, and many other times during the day.

Put a warm body next to mine, and I was ready. I would snarl derisively, "What's wrong with you?" As you can imagine, those interactions did not end well, and those words would come back to haunt me.

Flip forward a few years. I was in a relationship with a beautiful woman who was ready to have sex whenever I was. It was a dream come true. Either I initiated sex and she was ready and willing, or she initiated sex and I loved it.

And then one night, you probably know what's coming (or not), it happened! Teri snuggled up close and reached down for my penis. She couldn't find it (maybe she should have looked out of the window). After a few more unsuccessful attempts to get a reaction, she turned over and went to sleep. I stared at the ceiling feeling bad about myself.

We didn't talk about it. Not talking about upsets or anything having to do with feelings had become part of our relationship. For example, one day I was in my office when a friend sent a fax of the poem, "The Invitation" by Oriah Mountain Dreamer.

I was deeply moved by its simplicity and how so much of it spoke to me. I rushed upstairs to share it with Teri. She gave it a cursory read and with a blank stare gave the sheet back to me with a perfunctory "That's nice."

"How did you feel about it?" I tentatively asked.

"Like I said, it was nice. What's there to talk about?" And thus ended that.

That was typical of anything that had to do with feelings. I had noticed this but had pushed it to the back of my mind. After being married to a woman who had always wanted to talk about feelings, I did not mind this respite.

Not feeling turned on was not a one off. It started to happen more and more. As I became more passive, she became more overt, wearing sexy lingerie, rubbing up against me, and stroking my body.

She became unhappier, and I questioned my masculinity (obviously to myself). After our unsuccessful attempts to have sex, I would lie unresponsive thinking, "One of your most persistent fantasies since your teens has been having a woman come on to you. You've always had to be the aggressor. Now here she is, the gorgeous woman you've dreamed about lying next to you, naked, wanting you, and you're not turned on. What's wrong with you?"

When I, someone who had always been resistant to being in therapy, suggested that perhaps we should see a therapist, she adamantly refused. She said that she didn't believe in therapy and I shouldn't be so sensitive. We became more and more distant, and before long, we went our separate ways.

A few years later, I realized that during that relationship something in me had begun shifting away from the young buck that was always ready for sex with whomever and wherever. I had become more of the person that I described in chapter 2, "Emotional Evolution." My sexuality, which for most of my life had had been completely divorced from my feelings, had evolved. Keeping my heart on was now an integral part of my sexuality.

I thought back to what the woman had said to me about needing an emotional connection to fire her sexuality. I realized that there was in fact nothing wrong with her. Unlike the years of training that had separated my sexuality from my emotions, her sexuality had not suffered the same disconnection. Every time I think of how I made her wrong, I feel a pang of sadness.

As my self-doubt ebbed, I wondered what difference it would have made had I not been raised in a culture where in movies, magazines, and everyday conversation sex was portrayed as just a physical response. As I evolved, I began to really like this new part of me, and new horizons dawned.

> **LB:** *I need a sexual relationship to feel fulfilled.*
> **EB:** *Only when I can find fulfillment in many ways does sex not become addictive.*

Sex had become my respite from the world. My anxieties were quieted, and I could flow joyfully, freely, and spontaneously. It was the only place where I consistently experienced a sense of well-being.

Orgasm, not only mine but also of my partner, was the height of physical pleasure. Orgasm left me spent and at peace. Is it any wonder why I wanted to return to it often? The problem was that, with the sexual experience being the only place that left me with these feelings, I became obsessed with returning to it.

Typically, within a short time after a sexual experience, I would be thinking about the next time. In between sexual experiences, I would be planning how to get my fix. If it meant wooing her, I wooed her. If it meant bribing her, I bribed her. If my partner was not interested, I would engage in trying to get her in the mood. To achieve my goal, I developed a full arsenal of techniques from threats and guilt to promises and sweetness.

My sexual obsession was the motivation to be a good sexual student. I copiously read books and took classes on sexuality. The upside was becoming a better technician. The downside was adding more ammunition to make her wrong when she wasn't as interested in sex as I was.

I would have liked to make love every day if she had been willing. Although sex was one of the few times in our relationship that I experienced my compassion, joy, playfulness, and serenity, it became a constant source of fights and unhappiness. Eventually, it was one of the major issues that led to the end of the relationship.

After much deliberation, I realized that to heal the place in me that relied on sex as a way to connect I needed to give up sex for a while. The thought terrified me. I had thought about sex constantly since I was a teenager.

My sexuality and relationship neediness were both rooted in dependency. For years, I had felt somewhat superior to the drug and alcohol addicts that I treated because I was not dependent on those substances. The most humbling experience of my life was acknowledging that the only difference between us was our drug of choice.

Like any addict, when I finally admitted my addiction, I had to swear off my drug until I resolved the cause of my addiction. That meant learning how to create a sense of well-being that was not dependent on something outside myself.

From my work with addicts, I knew that when faced with this dilemma many people turned to different sources outside themselves for their sense of well-being, such as food, religion, sugar, television, or money.

I knew that before I would engage in sex again I needed to learn how to create my sense of well-being from within myself. Only in that way could sex take its place as an integral and healthy part of my life, rather than be an out-of-proportion, problematic part of my life.

When I mentioned to a few of my friends that I was going to become celibate, they thought I was crazy. Thankfully, by that time, I was in a men's therapy group. In sharing my sexual thoughts, feelings, and difficulties, I received support for my decision. In fact, two other men made the same commitment.

We continued to be a great support for each other during the times between group meetings and even after leaving the group. A few years went by before I felt ready to engage in a sexual relationship.

> **LB:** *Sex does not have to be loving to meet my needs.*
> **EB:** *Loving sex meets my need for emotional intimacy and is completely satisfying.*

During the summer of 1968 while on a trip to Europe, I visited a high school sex education class in Stockholm, Sweden. I welcomed this as part of my research for teaching a sex education class in the fall.

I was delighted by the comfort with which students and teacher discussed subjects that were taboo in United States such as sex aids, contraception, and abortion. I saw firsthand both about how far ahead of us they were and the possibilities of being so open about such an important subject.

After class, I had the opportunity to speak informally with some of the students. When everyone else had gone, three girls stayed behind to voice some of their concerns. They felt something was missing and were reticent to even talk about it.

As we talked, they realized what their uneasiness was about. Even with such openness in classrooms, in magazines, and on television, there was not much talk or understanding about the emotional and relationship aspects of sexuality. They feared they were alone in their distress.

Today, the freeing of sexual inhibitions has liberated both males and females to explore and experience some amazing potentials for sexuality. Yet the gnawing sense that those young women expressed is as relevant today as it was fifty years ago.

As a country, we have caught up with and surpassed most of the rest of the world in our openness about sexual materials and sexual enhancement techniques. Many ads on television proclaim the wonder of pills that produce erection, aids to stimulate orgasm, and enhancement surgeries for breasts or a larger sexual organ.

Most sexual discussions, however, still regard sex as merely a physical act. Conventional thinking is stuck in reducing sex to a performance. We have become better sexual gymnasts and experience more orgasms, but sexual activity seems to be merely reflecting a frantic search for the elusive prize of sexual satisfaction.

When I think back to those beautiful teenagers in Sweden yearning for something that was missing, it seems that we really haven't come that far. With all our talk, we are still a society that remains largely ignorant about the role of sex in bringing what we truly want. For the most part, almost nothing addresses the heart of sexuality, and so we remain clueless about complete sexual fulfillment.

> **LB:** *I must do many things to get her to have sex with me.*
> **EB:** *Satisfying sexual interactions grow naturally out of emotional intimacy.*

Most mornings I would wake up with an erection. I would cuddle her, stroke her body, fondle her breasts, and rub my penis against her leg. She typically would be distant and want to talk, often about the dreams she had during the night. The last thing I wanted to do was talk!

Many mornings she would subordinate her desire, and we would have sex. Sometimes, she would placate me by saying that we should wait until later. At night, when we got into bed, I was ready, and we would usually make love.

Whenever she would say that she didn't feel like making love, I would get really upset. I would try making her feel guilty with words such as "But you promised." Sometimes, that worked.

If it didn't work, I trotted out the bigger guns like "You made a commitment! How am I supposed to trust you if you don't keep your commitments?" Arguments over such things as what it meant to keep promises and make commitments would often follow.

Finally after many awful interactions, one or both of us would open to learning. In that light, we learned many important things. I looked at all the things I would do to manipulate a woman into having sex with me, whether wooing, cajoling, threatening, forcing, or guilting her.

Confronting those things made me feel awful about myself, but it opened the door to Evolving/Empowering Beliefs. I learned to have the faith that if we felt connected, sex would grow out of that emotional intimacy. I just had to show up with an open heart. If her heart was open, our closeness often led to lovemaking.

If her heart was not open and I cared about her, I would want to engage in finding out about her feelings. If she did not wish to engage and my heart stayed open, I would give her the space until she was ready.

> **LB:** *I should not need instruction in how to please my partner.*
> **EB:** *Only by communicating verbally or non-verbally can I know what is pleasurable for my partner in any moment of our sexual experience.*

I grew up believing that sex was a lights-out, no-talking, eyes-closed, quiet experience. Sex was an inward rather than a shared experience. It took a highly creative and artistic woman to free up my senses and expand the totality of my experience.

Sex became illuminated when she said, "Making love without light or with eyes closed is like standing blindfolded in front of a beautiful piece of art."

Under her tutelage I had only recently begun to appreciate fine art. Now, during sex, I opened my eyes, not only to the beauty around me but also and more importantly to her magnificence.

Since the eyes are the windows to the soul, looking into each other's eyes created a memorable heart connection. Seeing her naked body and how it looked when in the throes of ecstatic bliss was icing on the cake. The sound of her feelings was another wow! Hearing her delight in moans, heavy breathing, and squeals increased my arousal and guided me into knowing what was pleasurable and what was not.

Hearing Latin or classical music moved my body in sensual rhythm. Just as dancers allow music to move their bodies into creative expression, together we created our unique dance of love.

Since bodies change from day to day, assuming that I know what my partner wants is a trap. On any given day, one part of her body may feel wonderful when touched, and on another day, it may be numb.

Communicating during sex both heightens and directs the experience. Sharing our feelings about what we are experiencing or needing or not needing can be verbal or non-verbal cues. Such cues might include squirming, moving her hand faster or slower, or shifting from one place to another.

In my earlier relationships, I would touch my partner during foreplay because she liked it and it turned her on. I did not get much pleasure either from touching her or from being touched. In fact, I would always focus my touching on her breast and genitals and quickly push her hand down to my penis.

She suggested that if I learned to be more in the moment I might find greater pleasure in being touched. I was very skeptical but decided to go along with the program. To my surprise, I started to detect an increase in my pleasurable feelings.

Touch as a sensual, silky, and smooth caress gently glides along my body, bringing my skin alive. It differs from the touch of massage because it is so sensual. Over the next few years, my body opened more and more to touch. Eventually, my entire body became a sexual organ.

As I studied this phenomenon further, I discovered that what happened to me was not so unusual. At birth, our bodies are very sensitive, and being touched feels really good. But, as I grew up, I tended to shun touching, and pleasure got localized in my genitals. With the reversal of that charade, I reclaimed my body as the sensual organ it was designed to be.

As the pleasure I get from touching my partner has increased, touching her has changed from being something I do only for her to something that I do for myself as well. What a difference it makes when the pleasure I get is not just from giving pleasure but also from my own sensual delight.

> **LB:** *In a completely emotionally intimate sexual experience, it is possible to enjoy doing something that my partner does not find pleasurable.*
> **EB:** *When I am emotionally connected to my partner, I cannot find pleasure in doing something that my partner does not find pleasurable.*

I grew up with a breast fixation that *Playboy* magazine definitely encouraged. It was heaven when I finally hooked up with a sexual partner who had the perfect breasts. I knew that, although she did not receive pleasure from having her breasts ogled, caressed, or suckled, she tolerated it because I enjoyed it.

But it was never enough for me, and I always wanted more. As much as she tried to be a good sport, I sensed her annoyance or a distant tolerance more and more of the time. Eventually it became such an issue that it was a continuing source of unhappiness during sex.

It was not until I was in another relationship that an important awareness struck me. During a sexual experience in which I felt totally connected with my partner, I became aware that I was enjoying something that she was not. The good feelings immediately drained from my body. I became sad and our lovemaking stopped.

"What's going on?" she said.

"When I realized that you were not enjoying what I was doing, the thought of how often I had done that with you and others really hit me."

My confession touched her deeply. She realized how often she tolerated things being done to her that she did not like and how hard it was for her to stop it.

We held each other tightly and cried together as we recalled both the times when we allowed ourselves to be abused by enduring something that was not pleasurable and the times when we abused others by doing something that they did not like.

My life-changing realization was that when I am connected to my heart my sense of well-being is directly tied into my partner's well-being.

I cannot do anything that does not serve her. If she is not enjoying an experience, it is impossible for me to be enjoying it.

> **LB:** *The vagina is not beautiful.*
> **EB:** *The more I explore the vagina, the more I appreciate its depth and beauty.*

I grew up believing that the vagina was a rather unattractive part of a woman's body. In my youth, going down on a woman was the last thing I wanted to do. If a woman asked me to go down on her, I would dutifully accommodate. But I couldn't wait to come up for air as soon as it was safe to do so.

Years later, during my courtship with a woman, I admitted this for the first time. She said, "You're not telling me anything I don't already know. Why do you think I stopped asking you to do it?"

"Really," I said, "I thought I'd gotten pretty good at hiding how much I disliked it. You have to admit, the vagina is not very pretty."

With a slight nod and an understanding smile, she said, "You know, I grew up believing my vagina wasn't very pretty. I never thought it was ugly but certainly never thought it was beautiful. But that all started to change when I became acquainted with the artwork of Georgia O'Keeffe. If you've never seen her work, I'd love to introduce you to it."

Through her eyes, and O'Keeffe's art, I began seeing with new eyes. A new world opened as I related the curves and delicateness of O'Keeffe's flowers to my partner's vagina. I became fascinated by the wondrous complexity and contours within her vagina, the way its color would change and its mysterious depth.

Of course, as I became a connoisseur and loved spending more time with my new "friend," the experience opened up new possibilities for her sexual responsiveness. I had never continued to suck on a woman's vagina through her orgasm until I learned to love it.

Staying with her through her orgasm not only allowed the power of her orgasm to increase but also provided me with the ride of my life. Entering her as her orgasm was winding down brought new life into her experience. Our simultaneous orgasms often became a beautiful way to end the sexual part of our lovemaking.

> **LB:** *With aging, sex becomes less pleasurable and/or nonexistent.*
>
> **EB:** *Loving sexual experiences never get old, even as I do.*

As I've aged, my sexuality has certainly changed. In a recent relationship, we joked good-naturedly about how the sand that once formed beautiful hourglass figures had settled to the bottom. We noted how our skin, once as smooth as a baby's tush, was beginning to resemble the prunes that had become a staple in our diets.

My sexuality had definitely changed. The raging hormones, which once drove my sexuality like a NASCAR racer, now lounged in the back seat of a limo. The energy with which I once popped up in the morning and carried over into vigorous and athletic sexual encounters now had a slower rhythm and needed nap time to regenerate.

These issues brought up some troubling concerns. For her, being the aggressor was difficult for a woman trained to be a lady. For me, not responding to her overtures set off bells and whistles about getting old. I thought a good definition of old age might be waking up in the morning with the only thing stiff being the back.

After many discussions, we decided to try a popular drug designed to enhance male erections. Although the drug worked just fine, I felt uncomfortable and unsatisfied. "After all," I said, "if I'm not turned on enough to have intercourse, maybe my penis is telling me something that I should be listening to."

More good talks led to finding other ways to find sexual satisfaction that did not involve intercourse. We learned and really enjoyed new ways to use our fingers, tongues, and toes. But I was still not satisfied.

Continuing talks led to how much I had changed over the years in my ability to be more connected to my heart. "You know," I said, "even though I know it, it's sometimes still hard for me to admit how much my emotions are connected to my sexuality. Sex definitely has a different meaning to me than it had in the past. When I'm not feeling close and emotionally connected to you, I don't feel turned on. Do you know what I mean?"

She knew. With a good-natured pummeling of my head and chest with a pillow, we burst out laughing. The flame was ignited, and beautiful lovemaking ensued.

> **LB:** *Once a sexual experience begins, it ruins the mood to stop and discuss feelings.*
> **EB:** *Stopping to discuss feelings does not have to ruin a sexual experience.*

One time, before I realized that my sexuality was connected to my heart, losing my erection led to an amazing experience. I rolled over and stared silently at the ceiling.

Propping herself up on her elbow, Dawn ran her other hand caressingly through my thinning salt-and-pepper hair. She said, "Do you want to talk?"

"No!" I replied curtly.

"Okay, but just remember that I love you, and when you're ready, I would love to explore what's going on."

She lay back considering what she wanted to do until I was available. Switching on her nightstand night, she picked up a book, stuffed two pillows behind her head, and plunged into her novel. After a few minutes, she reached out to let me know she was available by placing her hand on my arm. I didn't respond, and eventually she withdrew it.

Another few minutes passed. Finally, I turned toward her and put my hand on her stomach. She reached down and cupped her hand over mine. I whispered, "I want to talk, but I'm scared."

Putting down her book and looking softly into my eyes, she said, "What's going on?"

"I'm scared that what I have to say may upset you, and I don't want to hurt you."

"I appreciate your concern, sweetheart, but you know that I'm learning to take better care of myself and I'm not so fragile. I can deal with my hurt. Is there anything else that you might be concerned about?"

I took a few deep breaths. I was having trouble looking her in the eyes. "I guess I'm also scared of how you're going to react. I know it's been a long time since you've withdrawn, but I'm still afraid that you might shut down."

She smiled lovingly. "Well, I guess we each still have our tender areas, but I'm ready to get into whatever comes up when you are."

I took some even deeper breaths. "A while ago when we weren't as close as we are now, I stopped feeling very turned on by you. I got into the habit of using fantasy to maintain my erection, but tonight I couldn't."

After a few seconds that seemed like minutes, she said, "That really hurts, and I am pissed. I know there's pain underneath my anger, but right now I feel like I just want to beat the shit out of you."

I felt compassion and thought I could maintain a loving space while she vented her anger. "I knew you would be upset, and I'm ready to hear your anger, so have at me."

She really let loose, screaming at me and other men with whom she had been involved for keeping her down and now telling her that she wasn't attractive enough. She blamed herself for being such a wimp and this crazy-making culture for giving her the messages about her body and her sexuality that filled her with so much fear. All this and more she spewed all over me.

As it spilled out, rather than taking it personally and thinking about what I was going to say in defense, I just listened and felt her deep pain. As she started winding down, my sadness started building.

Finally, with her magazine of anger spent and lying harmlessly between us, her sadness bubbled forth. When she looked at me and saw my caring and vulnerability, her dam burst. We collapsed into a very moist embrace. As we each felt the pain from the past, we silently held each other for a long time. So much had been stirred up that it was hard to talk.

Our silence was broken, and I just held her while she cried over her missed opportunities to develop her many unique talents and abilities. Then she held me as I felt and explored the pain of contributing to her self-doubts with my criticism.

Our exploration lasted for hours. At 1:00 a.m., as we lay exhausted in each other's arms, I became aware of how good it felt to have my limp penis touching her leg. I noticed my tiredness lifting. When I moved my hand to gently touch her breast, my penis began feeling even better and more alive.

As we caressed each other with our mouths and tongues, her sexual feelings began stirring. Her hand reached for my penis. We looked at each other and smiled playfully. I said, "Wait a minute. I'll be right back."

I quickly put a CD in the stereo, pushed the play button, and hurried back to bed. As our favorite romantic music filled everything and every body in the room, we resumed our horizontal dance.

As I deeply experienced my love, I noticed a pang of fear. I decided to let it go, but made a mental note to explore that fear with her at another time. For now, I just wanted to immerse myself in her beauty and our love.

Being fully present and turned on to her produced wonderful feelings. Looking into her eyes, I experienced her magnificence. True, she had always been beautiful to me, but this time, I saw beyond the physical into the special place where the unadulterated soft and innocent person resided.

The music informed my hands, and depending on where the notes directed them, they circled or stroked, lingered or roamed, played or caressed. I entered her easily and gently with a shudder that coursed through my entire body.

The mixture of passion and serenity felt like coming home. We didn't move. We just looked at each other, allowing the delicious feelings of ecstasy to fill every part of our bodies.

Although our subsequent explorations did not always end in a sexual experience, our talking very often was lovemaking. At those times, each of us felt completely satisfied as we fell asleep in each other's arms, filled with appreciation for having each other on this journey.

Even though we had gotten back to the good stuff, I clung to the notion that I just got lucky and that returning to sex was the exception to the rule. It took a few more times for another false belief to bite the dust.

Without a doubt, talking about problems turns off sexual feelings. Especially when we get knocked off center and the discussion deteriorates into an upsetting interaction.

With the patience and caring that accompanies willingness to learn, we return to our hearts. Compassionate listening allows us to feel heard and reconnect emotionally. This level of intimacy leaves us feeling cared about and complete. In such an atmosphere, sensual sexual passion returning is the rule, rather than the exception.

> **LB:** *Over time, sex naturally becomes routine and less frequent.*
> **EB:** *Sex is forever creative when we are giving and receiving in the moment.*

Conventional wisdom taught me that in an on-going relationship sex becomes routine over time. The new dimensions that heartfelt conversations can bring to a relationship make that idea obsolete. The more we learn about ourselves and unburden ourselves from the sexual baggage we carry, the closer we get and the more delicious becomes our sex life.

When sex is not used to get or prove something, making love becomes deeply meaningful and intimate. My partner and I then experience what we really want and need—a satisfying connection that is driven, not by need but by giving and receiving love.

A sexually intimate experience that flows from open hearts looks and feels entirely different from sexual experiences that are not heart connected. Lovemaking is not a race. Rather than running, we are dancing, creating many different and often unexpected forms on our unique journey in lovemaking.

Whatever happens is a result of clear verbal and non-verbal communication. There are no preconceived ideas of what a successful sexual experience would be, such as a simultaneous orgasm or even orgasm itself. There is never a predetermined finish line. I may reach the finish line ahead of her. We may reach it simultaneously. Or one or both of us may decide on a different finish line.

With no goal, there is only the moment. Being totally present in the moment determines the next moment. The route we take weaves its path, depending on what each of us discovers in each moment. In this way, the route is never the same, no matter how many times we do the dance.

The intimacy that results from talking and listening opens our hearts, and we connect heart to heart. When it involves our genitals, it is sexually intimate lovemaking. When it does not involve sexuality, it is still lovemaking, deliciously intimate, and often healing.

{ CHAPTER 4 }

# SPIRITUAL EVOLUTION:
## Living in the Mystery and Being Love

SPIRITUALITY WAS NOT PART OF MY YOUNGER LIFE. Jewish holidays were a drag. My grandfather, a very religious Jew who served as a cantor in his shul, went on and on in a language that I did not understand. Or I was dragged off to religious services that were completely useless to me.

At eleven years old, I was enrolled in Hebrew school to study for my bar mitzvah. All I wanted was to be playing after school. Instead, I was in classes that had no meaning or value to me. After my bar mitzvah, I vowed never to set foot in a synagogue again.

Enter the New Age of the 1960s. Gurus, television evangelists, workshops, best-selling books all proclaimed the spiritual path, including spirit guides, angels, past lives, reincarnation, and life after death.

I was with a woman who jumped into many of these beliefs with both feet. Typically skeptical, I either went along dragging one foot or completely pooh-poohed the idea. Many battles took place around her involvement and my resistance.

As many of our friends got caught up in one spiritual philosophy or another, I felt more and more alone. That loneliness began to end the day that my spiritual journey began.

> **LB:** *Spirituality does not require believing in unknowable concepts.*
> **EB:** *Spirituality is becoming a more loving person.*

I'll never forget that June morning I pulled out of my driveway at 4:30 a.m. I waved goodbye to the house I had lived in and loved for twenty years, the woman I had been married to for a quarter of a century, and a long and successful career as a psychotherapist. The mixture of stark terror and hopeful excitement was like nothing I had ever felt.

Unlike many of the confident movie heroes of my childhood, who conquered the West and rode off into the sunset, I unsurely rode into the sunrise. It was as if I was in an "Eastern." I felt more like "Wrong Way" Corrigan than John Wayne.

On a highway in Southern Utah, for the first time in my life, I drove off the main road and literally took the road less traveled. Alone, meandering through Zion National Park and Bryce Canyon, I was awestruck by a power and magnificence I had never before experienced.

Troubling questions, pain, doubt, and joy merged with the grandeur of nature's sculptures. A floodgate opened, releasing torrents of tears, both of gratitude and fear. The terror of leaving all the people on whom I had come to depend for emotional support and the sadness of ending a relationship with the only woman with whom I had ever been in love took a back seat to the exhilaration of launching a great adventure.

I began a new life in the mountains of Colorado. Living in a small town connected me to the earth and to people in an entirely new way.

Not long after settling in, I attended a workshop led by Jean Houston. An author, philosopher, and researcher in human capacities, Houston is regarded as one of the principal founders of the human potential movement. For two and a half incredible days, she led experiences that put us into the life and consciousness of Saint Francis of Assisi.

At the end of the workshop, under a brilliant clear and sunny umbrella, I drove up to the fourteen-thousand-foot serenity of Maroon Bells. Still in the consciousness of Saint Francis, I walked along Maroon Lake until finding an isolated spot. I sat down under a full-leafed aspen tree, closed my eyes, and thought about Saint Francis and his connection to nature and animals.

To my astonishment, when I opened my eyes, some of those wild animals were all around me. Squirrels scurried over my outstretched legs; two deer stood within a few feet looking at me, and birds perched on the limbs of the tree above me. One even came onto my shoulder. I had never been so close to wildlife before, and I just smiled in gratitude for this connection.

Upon returning to town, a few of my friends from the workshop gathered to watch *Brother Sun, Sister Moon*. The film is about Saint Francis and his evolution from a spoiled rich kid to someone connecting deeply with unfortunate people and nature.

The scene that particularly struck me was when Saint Francis renounces the life of wealth and privilege into which he had been born and proclaims his spirituality:

> I want to be happy. I want to live like the birds in the sky. I want to experience the freedom and the purity that they experience. The rest is of no use to me. If the purpose of life is this loveless toil we fill our days with, then it is not for me. There must be something better. There has to be. Man is a spirit; he has a soul. That is what I want to recapture, my soul. I want to live. I want to live in the fields. Stride over hills. Climb trees. Swim rivers. I want to feel the firm grasp of the earth beneath my feet without shoes, without possessions, without those shadows we call our servants.

Saint Francis has been a great inspiration in helping me connect to my essence. I have watched the film many times, and it never ceases to touch me deeply.

Understanding the heart as my essence means that it influences every aspect of my life—my feeling, thinking, willing, and seeing. When connected to my heart, I can connect in satisfying ways to others and to the mystery that is beyond humanness.

For the first time since high school, I established a best friendship with a male. The profound learning that accompanied my friendship with Lee Shapiro permeated my evolution toward learning to find my heart and recapture my soul.

One day while on a chairlift, Lee and I began one of our routine philosophical discussions. Still deeply engrossed when we reached the top of the run, Lee gestured toward the out-of-bounds fence and suggested we talk for a while. We skied to a deserted spot, took off our skis, and sat on a snow-covered rock.

I continued where we had left off. "You know, the more I allow things to unfold and don't try to plan everything or have control over things, the more peaceful I feel. Do you know what I mean?"

"Well, I'm not sure because I haven't known you for that long. But do you mean you're feeling more open and less defensive?" Lee asked.

"Yeah. It seems like the more open I am, the more secure I feel. I think that the more I know that I'm not dependent on anything or anyone outside myself for my sense of well-being, the more I'm gaining a faith that I've never known before."

Seeing that I was deep in thought, Lee didn't respond, and we sat quietly for a few minutes. Finally, I continued, "You know, I feel a humility in knowing that there are many things beyond my ability to know, and it doesn't matter. I think that the most important thing is just being the most loving person I can be.

"If there's a heaven, being open and loving should be enough to get me there. And if this lifetime is all there is, then so be it. I'm feeling so good that I wouldn't change a thing."

"Wow," Lee responded. "For a Tuesday morning at the top of the mountain, that's pretty deep, dude."

We looked at each other and started laughing. I really appreciated the way Lee allowed his learning to stay focused while he brought lightness into even our weightiest discussions. The thought of two men deeply sharing their thoughts and feelings caused my head to nod slightly in disbelief.

We buckled our boots, stepped into our skis, and began poling back toward the top of the ski run. I said, "Another thing I just thought of: some people used to accuse me of not being on a spiritual path because I didn't believe in things like past lives, spirit guides, and angels. I'm beginning to think that maybe it's just that our paths are different and that neither of us is right or wrong."

"Your path is definitely unique," Lee responded, "and that can probably be said of most, if not all, of us. I don't know what spirituality is, but it seems to me that playing God by pretending to know things that only God could know definitely doesn't seem spiritual."

As I thought about this, I realized that staying open and loving with others and truly respecting their beliefs as just as true as mine would make a great difference in my life. I thought, *Maybe living with that kind of humility is my spiritual path.*

I wanted to share this with Lee, but musing had slowed me considerably. Lee, an expert skier, was already at the Black Diamond sign that signaled an advanced run. He yelled over his shoulder, "I'm going to ski the bumps. I'll meet you at the bottom."

With a "yahoo!" he took off and disappeared from sight. I smiled as I tucked my last thought away in my "to be shared later" file. As confirmation that my path was different, I took off down a leisurely slope, silently slithering in six inches of new powder while fully reveling in the glow of the glistening, snow-covered branches.

The importance of connecting to one's heart is traditional wisdom, transcending any single religion and common to all. Not following any single religion allows me to study and take the best from many different sources. It allows more of the sacred connections that have created greater harmony and balance, pierced the veil of my separateness, and made me more complete.

One Sunday, a friend asked me to accompany him to a small, rather isolated church in Snowmass Village. Being in those simple surroundings and hearing Rev. Thomas Keating speak was eye and mind opening.

Fr. Keating was an American Catholic monk and known as one of the principal developers of Centering Prayer. I purchased his book, *Open Mind, Open Heart,* and was very inspired by his description of contemplative prayer. I began practicing this meditation that asks you to focus on something that represents love. I chose to meditate on light.

I had been meditating on light for about a month when, during one session, a figure began appearing in the light. As it came closer and more into focus, I recognized it to be Jesus. I was shocked.

Shaking my head, I thought to myself, *What are you doing in my meditation? I'm not even Christian. In fact, my grandfather was a rabbi, and if he knew you were here, I don't think he would be too pleased.*

Perplexed, I drove out to Snowmass Village to seek counsel from Father Keating. I told him what had happened and asked what he thought. Wisely he said, "I can't tell you the meaning of what happened to you. But just live with it, and the meaning will be become clear."

So began learning about Jesus. Being raised as a Jew and rarely even hearing his name, I began studying the life of Jesus without any preconceived ideas. I became fascinated with the pre-Easter Jesus.

Jesus became a model for how to respond with heartfelt feelings, regardless of the situation. When I was in difficult situations, I began asking myself, *How would Jesus respond?* The results were fantastic.

One of the authors who profoundly added to my knowledge was Marcus Borg, Hundere Distinguished Professor of Religion and Culture at Oregon State University, a member of the Jesus Seminar, and a major figure in historical Jesus scholarship.

His books spoke volumes to me. In *Meeting Jesus Again for the First Time*, Borg states, "For Jesus, compassion was the central quality of God and the central moral quality of a life centered in God. The crystallization of Jesus' message, 'Be compassionate as God is compassionate,' speaks of a way of life grounded in an *imitatio dei*, an imitation of God. To be compassionate is what is meant elsewhere in the New Testament by the somewhat more abstract command 'to love.'"

As I continued my spiritual studies, compassion became a central focus. The power of compassion became clear when I answered the following question: Who is powerful, people who close their hearts and strike back out of fear they will lose something or those who stay connected to their hearts and maintain their openness?

I thought of a take-off on the oft-quoted Rudyard Kipling poem, "If." It challenges us to keep our head when all about us are losing theirs. Substitute "heart" for "head," and therefore keeping my heart when all about me are losing theirs is the power I'm talking about.

I became fascinated with those people who did not have to be controlling because they came from a place of sureness inside themselves. The power that comes with that sureness is awesome. That is how I wanted to be. I did not want to try to control others or myself, either subtly or overtly. I wanted to be able to stay centered in any situation, no matter how anyone else behaved.

I began searching for both women and men, real or fictional, to serve as role models to help me stay connected to both my strength and my love. When I found such persons, I brought each into my meditation and imagined him or her as my guardian angel, there to help me learn to become more of the person I want to be.

The day I met one of my role models who embodied compassion both in his personal life and in his teaching sent me over the moon. I had moved to Oakland, California, and was dating a woman who lived in San Francisco. Every Sunday morning, she would walk the two blocks from her apartment to attend service at Grace Cathedral. I began staying with her on Saturday nights and going to church on Sunday.

Grace Cathedral is the fifth largest gothic cathedral in the world and is awesome in its own right. That alone made Sundays a spiritual adventure. Plus, every Sunday, Dean Alan Jones presented a wonderfully inspirational sermon.

One Sunday, Nobel Peace Prize winner Bishop Desmond Tutu spoke in Dean Jones's place. As Bishop Tutu talked about the South African Reconciliation Project, human rights and forgiveness, I was transfixed and transported.

As is the custom in the Episcopal Church, communion is given at the end of the service. In the past, when Karla would go for communion, I would stay seated. But on this Sunday, I just wanted to be close to such a man.

I looked up toward the heavens, and asking my grandfather for forgiveness, joined the line to take my first (and last) communion. And I wasn't disappointed. As I kneeled in front of Bishop Tutu, he touched my shoulder and our eyes met deeply. I burst into tears. I have never felt that way before or since in anyone's presence. I knew what spirituality looked and felt like.

During my time in the Bay Area, I began attending Spirit Rock Meditation Center and studying Buddhism with Jack Kornfield, a bestselling author and teacher in the *vipassana* movement in American Theravada Buddhism.

In his book *A Path with Heart*, Kornfield poses some questions with which to evaluate a spiritual community that I read over and over:

- Are you asked to violate your own sense of ethical conduct or integrity?
- Is there a dual standard for the community versus the guru and a few people around him?
- Are there secrets, rumors of difficulty?
- Do key members misuse sexuality, money, or power?
- Is there something powerful going on that may not really be loving?
- Is there a sense of intolerance?
- Is the community based on sectarianism or separation or does it have a fundamentalist quality to it?
- Am I becoming more isolated, dependent, obnoxious, lost, or addicted?
- Is there a greater capacity to know what is true for myself to be compassionate and tolerant?

Kornfield also gives a description of a spiritually mature person, which I use as a wonderful standard for evaluating my spiritual evolution:

> The spiritually mature person has learned the great arts of staying present and letting go. Their flexibility understands that there is not just one way of practice or one fine spiritual tradition, but there are many ways. It understands that spiritual life is not about adopting any one particular philosophy or set of beliefs or teachings, that it is not a cause for taking a stand in opposition to someone else or something else. It is an easiness of heart that understands that all of the spiritual vehicles are rafts to cross the stream to freedom.

As my spiritual journey continues, I have come to greatly appreciate the cultural aspects of Judaism that has so infused my sense of humor and capacity for empathy.

Rabbi Zalman Schachter-Shalomi was instrumental in bringing me back to my roots and embracing the spirituality of Judaism—the heart that got lost in my ritualistic upbringing. In *Jewish with Feeling*,

Reb Zalman says, "A spiritual seeker is a person whose soul is awake. Such a soul is not content to stay on the level of mere observance, ritual, and dogmatic belief. It needs a more personal and mystical approach. It senses the divine just beyond the surface of everyday existence and wants to connect to that."

My most profound teachers all taught what I believe is the essence of all major religions and spiritual disciplines, living a more heartfelt life. All heartfelt feelings and behaviors are spiritual experiences. (A partial list of them is in the appendix on page 106.)

> **LB:** *Holding beliefs rigidly keeps me safe.*
> **EB:** *Safety is an illusion, and holding beliefs lightly allows living in the mystery.*

It is hard to imagine a formalized religion or spiritual movement holding its beliefs lightly. Typically, such disciplines are based on the teachings of an "enlightened" authority that purport to be the truth. These ideas are detailed in books that are to be continually contemplated, if not memorized. Institutional movements thrive on attracting devotees who want an infallible source to reveal the information that will make everything turn out all right.

There is no doubt that putting out an idea as *a* truth does not carry the magnetism of beliefs that are put out as *the* truth. However, the important criteria for facilitating evolution of heart and soul cannot be met when there is only one truth.

My personal evolution is facilitated when spiritual teachings support my ability to discover meaning and truth for myself. This was much more commonplace in the past. Modern inventions from the printing press to television serve the mania for homogenizing differences and sacrificing individual thinking to "authoritative" analysis.

Consider that before the printing press, scriptures were read at public gatherings and discussed in small groups for clarity and finding meaning and truth for oneself. The invention of the printing press not only allowed mass distribution but also facilitated including interpretations that were to be learned and accepted on faith.

Traditional religions are easy targets for illustrating authoritarian-based ideas that separate people from heartfelt feelings and other people. Outside mainstream disciplines are persuasions that claim to offer alternative ways of embracing spirituality without the dogma of traditional religions but often miss that mark.

*A Course in Miracles* is an example of how even New Age philosophies can be authoritarian and thus frustrate spiritual evolution. I choose to exemplify this idea with *A Course in Miracles*, even though it is a philosophy with a basically positive message. Although I gained great value from it, it still contains some subtle assumptions that perpetuate Limiting Beliefs.

*A Course in Miracles* was written by a woman who purportedly channeled a voice that identified itself as the spirit of Jesus Christ. Nothing could be more authoritarian. For who could argue against a disembodied spirit with the credentials of a traditional God? If one were to hold that one's inner voice says something quite different, then what?

There is no doubt that *A Course in Miracles*, as with almost every religious and spiritual discipline and teacher, contains many wonderful and supportive ideas. However, being given truths without the caveat that they are merely chosen beliefs, or not being allowed to discover what is true for oneself, creates dependency, encourages a false righteousness, and ultimately blocks personal evolution.

Since many disciplines and spiritual teachers participate in truth selling rather than truth telling, it is up to me to gain the strength to see past their limitations, gather up the best they offer, reject what offends my self-trust, and seek support from like-minded spiritual seekers.

To facilitate my everyday evolution, the most important question through which to filter my experiences with religious/spiritual disciplines is "Does the discipline address my desire to rely on authorities and does it help me overcome this tendency?" An exercise for recognizing how rigidly held beliefs affect your life can be found in the appendix.

The juice of everyday evolution comes from the mystery of life working its magic. Without fear encasing my heart, I freely engage in the fullness of the moment. Captivated in the wonder of a fascinating adventure, I enjoy its surprises and challenges, rather than attempt to protect myself from potential difficulties. I feel alive instead of bored, passionate instead of dead, serene instead of anxious. I am animated instead of blasé and active instead of passive.

Heartfelt feelings empowering my abilities open me to new possibilities. Phenomenal awe-inspiring experiences that accompany living in the mystery are sometimes labeled magic or miracles—but they routinely happen when my heart is open.

The receptivity of an open heart can be symbolized by the image of outstretched arms with the palms turned toward the heavens. In this image, fear is not predominant, and the innocence and openness of living in the mystery is accompanied by softness, acceptance, and curiosity. It is a safe space for all thoughts, feelings, and actions.

Differences are welcomed and honored. Questions and problems are important, but rather than being treated as burdens, they are embraced as opportunities.

Expanding my time in the mystery brings me face to face with my most formidable obstacle—my mind. Part of a commitment to living in the mystery more of the time requires learning what it means to become more comfortable swimming in a sea of questions, rather than standing rigidly on islands of concrete beliefs.

The myriad things beyond my capacity to know with absolute certainty are part of the mystery of life. That mystery is illuminated by innumerable questions such as:

- What is the essence of human beings and of life itself?
- What behavior is right, and what is wrong?
- What things lie beyond my consciousness and my ability to perceive with my senses?
- What causes illness, and what heals us?
- What happens after death?

And, of course, the ultimate mystery from which the answers to many unknowable questions are drawn is: Who and/or what is God?

Since the loss of heartfelt feelings is directly affected by my beliefs and how I hold them, the quest for more Evolving Beliefs is greatly influenced by how I handle the unknowable.

I believed that I was accepting of differences. But once I discovered a truth, it was uncompromising. Therefore, anything else was not the truth. My way was the right way, and those who did not see things that particular way were misinformed and, therefore, wrong. If there is only one truth, how could it be any other way?

Beliefs like "There are no coincidences," "Whatever happens to you is part of God's plan," or "After you die, you go into the light and then . . . [fill in the blank here]" are opinions that can be comforting and can have a positive effect on one's life. However, when these beliefs are held as fact, distance and alienation from those who do not share those opinions are inevitable.

I heard a popular motivational speaker say in one of his seminars, "Whenever my wife and I are having difficulties with our children, we tell them that everyone chooses the family they are born into." This concept is not expressed as an idea but as a fact.

But how can he be sure? And, if he is speaking the truth, what does it say about those who do not believe they chose their family? Or when those in his audience accept the idea that we choose our birth family as the truth, what happens when it is expressed to others who do not believe it? This seemingly innocuous example illustrates some of the potential difficulties caused by teaching beliefs as if they are facts.

Once answers to unanswerable questions are believed to be the truth, it is a short step to attempting to convince others to believe it. But even if I do not attempt to impose my beliefs on others, holding them as universal truths rather than personal truths immediately disconnects me from the compassionate acceptance and respect of my heartfelt feelings.

When living in the mystery, I gratefully and humbly accept any information I am given without the necessity of naming it and creating a story about where it came from. Dreams, voices, and visions are gifts and wonders to be used in whatever way serves me in becoming more loving.

I can have fun with the information and play with the myriad possibilities of where they may have come from. As soon as I become attached to a particular interpretation, I leave the mystery and become subject to the arguments and the distance that result from rigidly held beliefs.

Being freed from trying to determine a single truth allows appreciation for the gift of divergent views that I have been given. Just imagine a world where religions hold their doctrines as choices, rather than as God-given or divinely inspired absolute truths.

Holding beliefs as choices, not facts, acknowledges that they are a subjective reality, which I have chosen. "I choose to believe there are spirit guides" is very different from "There are spirit guides." When lightly held, beliefs are not attached to sanctity but acknowledged as my truth, not the truth.

The Indian spiritual guru Jiddu Krishnamurti said, "The highest form of human intelligence is the ability to observe without evaluating." When living in the mystery, although solutions are not the focus, meaningful answers come naturally and effortlessly. These answers are not taken as gospel but are seen as transitory. They are merely door openers for other questions.

Inhabiting the unknown and constructing ideas to explain the unexplainable are understandable. In the face of fears that lie in the unknown, using my intellect in an attempt to feel safe makes perfect sense. But there is a price to pay—my attempts to have control over life block the flow that connects me to my heartfelt feelings, to others, and to Spirit.

Living in the mystery and letting go of control is living with humility and faith. Bringing my beliefs into alignment with my heartfelt feelings and developing the courage to live in the mystery and be love is my never-ending spiritual evolution.

{ CHAPTER 5 }

# INTELLECTUAL EVOLUTION:
## Being Smart Has Nothing to Do with IQ

FROM BEING A NINE-YEAR-OLD who didn't know the difference between a football and a baseball, I made myself into a pretty good athlete. I worked hard spending every free moment shooting hoops and watching radio (in the 1950s, there was not much sports on TV). I became the starting center on my high school basketball team and began my love of playing tennis. I had no interest in anything except sports.

Now, I have an embarrassing admission to make. Not thinking I was very smart and not studying in most of my classes, I resorted to cheating to pass my classes. Even with that, I barely made it through high school. At graduation, all my friends were admitted to four-year colleges; I was not. My only option was to slink off with my tail between my legs to Los Angeles Community College.

I don't know how I managed to get through those two years and my next two at UCLA. Graduating with a C-plus average, I was twenty-one years old and clueless about what I wanted to do when I grew up. At age twenty-eight, I was still clueless, was collecting unemployment insurance, had cheated to get through school with Cs, and had failed at four different careers. What was I to think?

> **LB:** *I am not very smart, and not thinking or speaking very easily or quickly is an indication of that lack of intelligence.*
>
> **EB:** *I have the capacity to nurture my ability to give and receive love, and I am fine if my thought process is slower and my verbal ability is less than others'.*

The direction of my life changed dramatically during the summer of 1963. On our third date, Margie suggested we see the film *Who's Afraid of Virginia Woolf?* We were not even out of the theater before she was bubbling over about how profound it was.

I interrupted her excitement. "The whole play was just two sick people yelling at each other. Halfway through, I fell asleep."

"How could you fall asleep?"

Tension mounted as we got into the car. Margie got so much meaning from the play. She had so much to say about it. I didn't understand it at all.

As we drove home in silence I thought about how different our reactions had been. "She is intelligent and insightful. I'm not. I like musical comedies and novels that are straightforward and easy to understand. She likes abstract art, and movies and plays that are heavy with symbolism." I never liked many of the things she did and always put them down with my standard response: "That's dumb."

It wasn't long before she came right out and said it. "I'm very much in love with you, but I'm afraid that as I continue to learn and grow, we'll get further and further apart. I need you to grow with me, find your passion, and bring me some intellectual stimulation."

Considering the possibility of going back to school touched into one of my deepest fears. I sheepishly admitted, "That terrifies me. I never thought I understood as much as other people." Looking away from her, I continued, "There's something else that I've never told anyone." Taking a deep breath I said, "I cheated in a lot of my classes just to get through."

Margie moved closer. Gently lifting my head, she looked into my eyes, saying, "I don't know what was going on then, but I think you're an intelligent person, and I'm sure you'll do well."

I applied to graduate school. After checking my transcripts, it was determined that I didn't have the grades. I was rejected. But after a conference with the dean of admissions, he decided to give me a chance. Frightened and unsure, I started back to school.

It didn't take long to realize that I had changed during the seven years since graduation. Learning was easier and more purposeful. I was in school because I wanted to be and I had a goal. As I dug into many issues, I became excited about education and about teaching. The more I succeeded, the more I believed in myself.

In my final semester I was required to take a class in improving my writing skills. Writing really terrified me. During my undergraduate years, I had studiously avoided all classes that required writing—term papers, essays, or anything other than true/false or multiple-choice tests.

On my first exam, I got a D. Luckily the professor seemed to like me and gave me some special attention. I struggled but managed to keep my head above water. For our last assignment, the professor told us to pick a play, read it and the reviews it had received, and then write our own review. I chose *Who's Afraid of Virginia Woolf?* I got an audio recording, bought a copy of the play, and went home to listen and read.

The play still seemed abstract, but I was determined to make sense out of it. The more I got to know the characters the more I felt that I understood why they behaved as they did. I read the reviews and listened a third, fourth, and fifth time. By the time I sat down to write my paper, I could see that the play brought out the difficulty of knowing what is truth and what is illusion. I could relate it to myself and to my relationship.

When I had first seen it, I was defensive because I didn't understand it. This time, I worked at it until I understood it. I felt a sense of excitement and pride. The better I knew the play, the better I liked it . . . and me.

I worked harder in that class than any other class. I improved my writing until I earned a final grade of B. Even though it spoiled my otherwise perfect record of straight A's, that B was the grade I was most proud of.

Doing well in school was not enough to quiet the nagging doubts about my intelligence. I was surrounded by people who thought and spoke much more quickly than I did.

One time I suggested to a dear friend that we watch a film we had just seen for a second time. She adamantly nixed that idea. She said, "I get irritated when I see a film more than once. I know everything that's going to happen. I even remember most of the dialogue."

My memory has never been great. I even have trouble remembering what I did last week. But I enjoy seeing a movie a second or even third time, not only to remember it but also to understand it on a deeper level. The first time through, I get caught up in the story and how it's going to end. The next time through, I see things that I completely missed the first time that help in that deeper insight.

Years later, I taught the idea that understanding something of depth might take reading or seeing things more than once. During one class period, I would show the film *The Fisher King*. At the film's conclusion, I would ask a series of questions. One such question was, "The song, 'How About You?' plays in part throughout the film and is sung in its entirety at the end of the movie. What is the meaning of the song and its relationship to the film?" My students were flummoxed.

I instructed them to see the film during the week between classes and write the answers to a few questions. At the next class, they came in buzzing with excitement. They were amazed at how much more they understood after seeing the film a second time. We had a stimulating discussion.

By the way, the answer to the question about the song is that the film is based on the idea that the simple things in life are what we need for our pleasure and sense of well-being. Knowing that, as you read the words of the song below, think of the feeling it creates in you and what the song means to you:

> I like New York in June, how about you?
> I like a Gershwin tune, how about you?
> I love a fireside when a storm is due.
> I like potato chips, moonlight and motor trips,
> How about you?
> I'm mad about good books, can't get my fill.
> And Franklin Roosevelt's looks give me a thrill.
> Holding hands in a movie show,
> When all the lights are low
> May not be new, but I like it,
> How about you?

In this fast-paced world, I like to operate at a slower pace. I like to connect more with my heart and this amazing environment that we have been given on earth. How about you?

I don't understand intellectually complex ideas very well and get confused by them. It took many, many years for me to accept that, rather than cluttering my mind with complex thoughts, I prefer simplicity. I think of my mind like my house. I like my house decorated simply, rather than filled with lots of things covering very square inch.

For years, I poured over complex ideas regarding human behavior. Finally, I distilled them down to the simple idea that our feelings and emotions can be divided into just two categories: heartfelt or protective feelings. And then I added that realizing when my feelings are heartfelt boils down to knowing if I'm feeling compassion and being open to learning. Pretty simple, isn't it?

At one time, I worked as a co-therapist with a colleague who seemed to dazzle clients with her ability to assess situations and prescribe solutions. I questioned my value as a therapist.

Years later I would occasionally meet ex-clients. Sometimes, they would tell me how much they appreciated and grew from my slower, more accepting demeanor of listening that left them feeling understood.

My intellectual evolution has meant realizing that intellectual brilliance is overrated. Being smart has nothing to do with IQ. The one essential quality that people closest to me value over my intellect and knowing a lot of stuff is my ability to listen with compassion.

> **LB:** *Giving advice is a good way of helping others.*
> **EB:** *Compassionate listening is the most important gift I can give to another.*

Anyone can be a compassionate listener. Listening compassionately is just listening with the big heart with which we all have been endowed.

Compassionate listening may sound easy, but it goes against almost everything that I had seen modeled. Typically, while one person was speaking, I remember my mind thinking of a response. Such thoughts might be offered as judgments about the other person's thoughts, feelings, and actions; solutions for the problem; or how they handled a similar situation. None of this demonstrated acceptance, understanding, and faith that a person could work out his or her own solutions.

When I am totally present with another, there is openness and appreciation for the feelings that are present. Compassionate listening involves learning about another person. It entails listening for the thoughts and feelings underneath what a person is saying and then reflecting back what I sense he or she is thinking and feeling.

A person may be angry, but if I sense the fear or sadness that his or her anger is covering, that is what I reflect. A person may be upset with a situation, but if I sense confusion, then that observation is what I share. The idea is to focus on hearing with ears connected to heart.

We all yearn to feel understood. Sharing difficult feelings and feeling thoroughly heard and completely respected are rare. It is compassionate listening that gifts another person with that experience. In this regard, some of the most useful and powerful words ever spoken were revealed centuries ago in the prayer of Saint Francis of Assisi: Seek not to be understood but to understand."

The title of the following (anonymous) poem is "Listen." Do you hear it?

> When I ask you to listen to me,
> And you start giving me advice,
> You have not done what I asked.

When I ask you to listen to me
And you begin to tell me why I shouldn't feel
 that way,
You are trampling on my feelings.

When I ask you to listen to me,
And you feel you have to do something to solve
 my problems,
You have failed me, strange as that may seem.
Listen! All that I ask is that you listen,
Not talk or do—just hear me.

When you do something for me
That I need to do for myself,
You contribute to my fear and feelings on inadequacy.

But when you accept as a simple fact
That I do feel what I feel, no matter how irrational,
Then I quit trying to convince you
And go about the business
Of understanding what's behind my feelings.

So, please listen and just hear me.
And, if you want to talk,
Wait a minute for your turn—and I'll listen to you.

> **LB:** *Learning about my Limiting Beliefs is unimportant.*
> **EB:** *Personal evolution must include learning and moving beyond my Limiting Beliefs.*

A defining characteristic of childhood is curiosity. Learning to walk, talk, socially interact, and a plethora of intellectual concepts is non-stop. But learning about myself, the reasons for my behavior, was never part of my life.

Learning about myself doesn't require a high IQ. In fact, super-intelligent people are so adept at creating rationalizations for their behavior that they often use their intellect to avoid looking at themselves.

Underlying the openness necessary for personal evolution to take place is the awareness that in any difficulty there is something valuable to be learned. This openness involves a sincere curiosity about myself, my world, and the people with whom I come into contact.

This inevitably brings me face to face with the parts of myself that have been repressed to avoid criticism and rejection, both my own and from others. Until these parts are confronted, I need to protect myself from having those parts touched or exposed. When the goal of protection is paramount, I cannot allow myself to experience what I fear.

One day, after an upsetting telephone conversation with Dawn, I rode my bike to Lee's frame shop. Lee immediately sensed something was wrong. "Hey, bud, you look like you could use a talk. Jerry can watch the shop. How about you and I go for a walk?"

We started down the Rio Grande Trail toward the river.

"What's going on?" Lee asked.

"I just had an awful interaction with Dawn. We were having a great talk until I said something about how I was learning not to get hooked into proving something was right or wrong and what a difference that was making in our interactions. Out of the blue, she says, 'I'm feeling uncomfortable right now. It feels like you're pulling on me.' Well, I lost it. I was just expressing my excitement, and she drops that same old crap on me. You know, sometimes I think she's just nuts. She's so damn unappreciative." I looked to Lee for approval of my evaluation of Dawn. I didn't get it.

"Seems like you're in some pain about that," Lee gently suggested.

With that, my anger drained, and my body lost some of its rigidity. I confessed, "Yeah, I feel she's always so defensive that she doesn't really see me. She thinks of me as such a bad guy, like I'm only after something for myself. She's even called me selfish and narcissistic. It feels lousy."

We had reached the river, and Lee suggested we wade out to a big flat rock that lay newly exposed from the retreating winter's thaw. Sitting in the middle of the river in the bright June sun with my best friend at my side felt like heaven.

And then he dropped the "Lee-shell": "Do you want some feedback?" he asked.

"Sure, I think," I said with a half-hearted attempt at some humor.

"Well, I don't think Dawn is crazy. Your conscious intent may not have been to get something from her, but my guess is that there was a part of you that wanted something. Can you think of anything else that may have been going on for you?"

I thought for a minute and then said sheepishly, "I was feeling a little lonely, and I guess I wanted to connect with her." After another pause I continued, "I also wanted her to know how well I'm doing. I guess her approval is still important to me." After a very brief pause, I added, "But I really was interested in finding out about her."

"I'm sure all those things are true," Lee said, "but she only picked up on the part that felt invasive. You know that setting boundaries has been an issue for her. But what does that tap into for you?"

"I guess it's hard for me to cop to all the different parts of myself. I still get hooked into the belief that I'm wrong if my intentions are not strictly honorable. And I guess I haven't made it okay to be selfish at times. But I am."

"I know," said Lee, "and I love you anyway." We reached out and hugged each other.

We continued chatting on our river oasis for a while longer before it was time to go.

When we stood up, Lee asked, "How are you feeling?"

"Much better," I replied. As I looked at him, I shook my head in gratitude for this man who, by modeling the ability to live in his heart rather than his head, had opened me to so many gifts that I might never have known.

{ Chapter 6 }

## Career and Creative Evolution:
Finding Passion and Being of Service

My sister began taking singing, dancing, and acting lessons at the age of three. At nineteen, she landed the female lead in a major Broadway musical.

I had a different trajectory. It didn't take a crystal ball to know that an NBA future did not look promising for a six-foot-tall white guy who couldn't jump high enough to touch the rim. A view from athletics to scholarship didn't show much promise either. Even though I had dutifully fulfilled the requirements of my college education, I found little value in it. I did my undergraduate work in psychology at a highly respected university. The only two schools of psychology that were taught were Freudian analysis and B. F. Skinner's behavioral model. With the only choices being to listen passively or study rats in a maze, I left college for the business world.

I was hired as a personnel specialist at a fledgling electronics company. Litton Industries was to become an international giant. A successful career there would have probably been satisfying. But at that time, the very compassionate and highly sensitive person with a strong desire to be of service to others had not yet emerged. Four highly undistinguished years later, I left my personnel career to begin training as a stockbroker.

After learning the technical aspects of the brokerage business, I was pronounced ready to be a salesman. Talk about a fish out of water! Without a strong connection to my internal compass, I had no idea that a business in which the only thing of importance seemed to be making money had little to offer me. Not surprisingly, I floundered while losing money for my family and friends (to whom else do you begin selling stocks?). Finally, the inevitable day arrived, and by mutual consent, the company and I parted ways. A salesman I am not.

My next opportunity was in the show-business crazy town of Hollywood. I produced a children's show. Although the show was pretty decent, I had no idea of the responsibilities of a producer. It and I were flops.

I was desperate. My father was about to begin building an eighteen-unit apartment building. He suggested teaching me the building business. Turns out my father, a painting contractor, was not the sharpest nail in the building world. Although we made a small profit, dealing with people who were either niggling to make more money or being very unreliable was not for me.

> **LB:** *I cannot make enough money doing what I love to do.*
> **EB:** *Finding and doing what I love will lead to making the money that I need.*

At twenty-eight, I was a failure at four different careers, collecting unemployment insurance, and without a clue as to what I was going to do when I grew up. I had known Margie just a short time when she asked, "Have you ever been happy doing anything at which you think you could make a living?"

"The only thing I've ever enjoyed doing was coaching the kids at the YMCA."

"Well, what about teaching?" she said.

"Are you kidding?" I shot back. "I've always thought I might like teaching but never seriously considered it. The pay is so bad. How can anybody be happy on a teacher's salary?"

I never expected the next words I heard. To this day, they are among the most important words anyone has ever said to me. "I don't think that we need much money to be happy, but I know that we don't have a chance of being happy if you're not fulfilled in your work. If you want to go into teaching, I'm behind you all the way. Besides, I'll be working, and we'll do okay."

One graduate school experience that stands out was my last class session before going out to teach. My professor delivered what he said was his most important lesson of caution. The hall was filled with excitement as he told the story of his best friend. He was a teacher who had befriended one of his students who was having family difficulties. The story arced through a drama-filled semester that ended with the student committing suicide. The teacher, devastated by the experience, went into a deep depression that eventually led to him leaving teaching. The poignant message and warning: "Don't ever become personally involved in the lives of your students."

I have often wondered how many prospective teachers were given and followed such an ominous warning. But being older than my fellow classmates, I didn't pay much attention to it.

In general, formal education is designed to push factual information and rote learning, to pass on established thinking, and to foster conformity. Innovative thinkers like Parker Palmer helped give me the courage to know that only education that does not stop at the neck but is integrated into the whole person allows both students and teachers to find real meaning and satisfaction from the experience.

In *To Know as We Are Known*, Palmer describes the lack of connection between teachers and students in the following way:

> From our [educated] platform we observe and analyze and assess, but we do not go into the arena—for that is how we have been taught to know. This means that virtues like compassion, the capacity to "feel with" another, are "educated away." In their place arises clinical detachment; counselors and physicians are trained not to get involved with their clients, journalists with their stories, and lawyers with their cases. Involvement has its problems, but is detachment the solution?

The moment I stepped into the classroom, I felt, for the first time in my life, at home. There, in my tiny high school classroom, I could connect to the compassionate person within and make a significant difference in the lives of my students. I had the freedom to be humorous, creative, and full of feeling. The more fully I allowed these aspects of my essence into the classroom the more successful I became.

The signature experience of my time in the classroom was my willingness to care deeply for my students' well-being. This often meant going beyond what I was charged with teaching them and into their personal lives.

My greatest challenge came in 1966, my second year of teaching health education. During a unit on drug education, one of my more surly students confronted me with "Have you ever tried drugs?"

I sheepishly admitted, "No, when I was in high school I had never even heard the word marijuana."

"Well," some of the longhaired, rather motley crew chimed in together, "why don't we teach you?"

So they talked and I listened. Near the end of the semester, the same group approached me after class and asked if they could talk with me after school. The conversation consisted of admissions that they were having some problems related to their drug use. In the end, they asked if I would be willing to talk about that outside of class time. I told them I had to think it over.

Not being a counselor, I sought the advice of Caldwell Williams, a seasoned counselor who was very popular amongst the students. He said that he too had received similar requests and suggested that we meet together with his students and mine. Thus began regular meetings where students had a sanctuary to talk, listen, and learn.

As the number of participants grew, it was only a matter of time until the administration heard about our new venture. We were summoned to the principal's office. Sitting on a brown wooden bench outside the clouded glass enclosed office felt like I was a high school student again. I anxiously waited for the ax to fall.

I was not disappointed. Our principal laid down the law regarding meetings outside of class time and forbade us to continue. As we left the office, I turned to Caldwell, shrugged my shoulders and said, "Well, I guess that's it."

He resolutely shot back, "No way, we're going ahead."

"Easy for you to say," I said with chagrin. "You have tenure. Not only do I not have tenure, but I have a small child at home."

When I got home, I told Margie what had happened. She said, "This is really important, and you have my full support. What's the worst that could happen? If you lose your job, we'll start over someplace else. It's not worth caving in to such uncaring thinking."

Caldwell and I continued our program, and I went back to school to learn more about counseling. D.A.W.N. (Developing Adolescents Without Narcotics) grew into one of the most successful drug prevention programs in the city.

Three years later, we were on stage at a city of Los Angeles awards program being presented with an outstanding service award. Our principal stood between us. Putting his arms around us, he proclaimed to the audience how he had supported us all the way. I smiled to myself and imagined both Caldwell and me suppressing the same urge to kick him.

I will be forever grateful for the support that helped me find the strength to challenge the conventional thinking of my professor, administrator, and some of the parents of my students. This gave me the opportunity to make a significant contribution to the lives of others at that time and beyond.

As a result of my success, the National Institute of Health commissioned a film to be made about my approach to teaching. That film was part of a program taught by the Social Service Seminar to teachers all over the country. I am told that *One Teacher's Approach* was the most controversial of the films and stimulated lots of discussion over the issue of whether teachers should go beyond protocol.

I know the controversy over any kind of emotional connection between teacher and student continues today. I was very judicious in how and with whom I would connect in this way. I have no doubt that education to be meaningful and effective must go beyond the head.

Upon getting the further training and credentials, I began my career as a psychotherapist. Although I enjoyed this work, being a high school teacher will always be my favorite job. It allowed me to express who I really am and be creative in how and what I taught. Even after a successful career in psychotherapy, were I to complete the sentence Jordan Paul is a . . ., it would not psychotherapist; it would be teacher.

After five years of being a therapist, the thought of writing a book came up. Margie had joined me as a co-therapist, and we felt we had some important things to say. Although that was true, writing seemed out of the question. I thought back to my time in school and how I had avoided any class that required written work. Now, here I was up against my strongly held belief that I could not write.

We plunged ahead into what was to become a really painful process. Not only did I not have a clue about writing techniques, but using a typewriter and having to struggle with carbon paper was frustrating and exhausting. With a lot of help from a wonderful publisher and editor, we got it done.

Completing the book brought the next terrifying task of doing promotional media interviews. The first interview was scheduled at a small college radio station that had an audience of probably ten people. Nevertheless, I'll never forget the stomach-churning feeling of diarrhea that accompanied the drive to that station. During the next few years, that same anxiety accompanied the first time I did more popular local radio and television programs. The crown jewel was finally getting booked to do my first national television appearance on *Good Morning America*.

Each new challenge became comfortable only after doing it a few times. Eventually I came to know that I am a really good speaker. But believing in my writing ability was more of a challenge (more about that later in this chapter).

Through it all, I have realized that finding satisfaction in my work has two main components. The first is finding my passion. It took me until I was nearly thirty to find mine is teaching. The second, being of service, is how I find ultimate satisfaction and meaning in whatever I am doing.

> **LB:** *Being of service is available only in certain professions.*
> **EB:** *Being of service is available in whatever I am doing.*

I grew up with a visceral fear of police officers. Walking into the office of Police Chief John Goodwin was totally intimidating. My body eased when I read the following framed quote by Martin Luther King that hung on his wall: "Not everybody can be famous but everybody can be great, because greatness is determined by service. What I know for sure is that whatever is done from the paradigm of service offers love and hope to those who receive it." As we talked, it became apparent that Goodwin was no ordinary chief of police.

The following year I was a featured speaker at John Denver and Tom Crum's annual conference, "Choices for the Future." I was given complimentary tickets and offered one to Goodwin. He eagerly accepted telling me that he had always wanted to attend the conference but couldn't afford the cost.

The focus of the conference was the environment, peace, and personal development. It was 1989, and many of us were aware of the crisis our environment was facing that still today many elected officials refuse to address. During the conference, I would look around the auditorium until I found Goodwin always sitting on the edge of his seat taking in every word.

At the end of the conference I caught up with him and asked, "How did you like the conference?"

"It was life changing. And don't tell anyone, but I realized that I'm not just the chief of police. I'm the chief of peace!" (I've told that to only about five hundred people, so beware of telling me something that I am not to repeat.)

Goodwin and I didn't become just friends; he became one of my dearest friends. During our many visits, we talked about how any activity whether at home or at work is an opportunity to be of service and make a positive difference in the lives of others. At the end of one discussion, Goodwin asked if I would be willing to conduct a workshop for the entire department to create an updated mission statement with that focus.

I was honored and went to work on creating the training. The workshop produced a magnificent mission statement that extolled the many beautiful values of being of service. It included the virtue of being respectful and a commitment to this value. The words were displayed on walls and talked about with pride.

However, even in the immediate afterglow of our hard work, I noticed that there was not much change in the everyday behavior around the organization. The situations that had been met respectfully continued, but the situations that had been met with disrespect continued as well. I was disappointed and perplexed.

One night, I awoke with what I thought was a great idea. Even though other such epiphanies paled in morning's light, this one continued to be exciting. I dropped by Goodwin's office and said, "Our beautiful words and ideals are not being matched by our actions."

I didn't have to go any further. He had observed the same thing and suggested we call the department together for a meeting.

I began the meeting with "For both patrol officers and administrative personnel, getting your tasks accomplished is essential. I propose that we now make being respectful to everyone involved as equally essential as completing our tasks and goals. For patrol officers, that means stopping a person who is breaking the law without compromising the integrity of either the lawbreaker or yourselves." As I spoke, I illustrated this with a mathematical formula, $R = T + G$.

At that point, a barrage of objections was hurled at me. "What if he has a gun?" "Certain people don't deserve to be respected." "We always treat people respectfully." My self-satisfied optimism quickly turned to shocking confusion.

In the discussion that followed, the officers discovered that although suspected lawbreakers were usually treated respectfully, this was not always the case. The most common realization was: "I've never thought about being respectful."

We began an ongoing process of confronting and learning how to walk our talk and live our values, rather than just talking about them. As we wrestled with the concept of respect, it became a challenge to learn from situations that produced disrespectful behavior and to find answers to questions like:

- What would have been the response that would not have compromised the other person's integrity or my own?
- What got in the way of behaving respectfully?
- What needed to happen to be able to respond respectfully?

Without making respect essential, these questions would, in all likelihood, never have been asked or answered. A list contrasting respectful and disrespectful behavior can be found in the appendix.

By making respect as important as accomplishing tasks and goals, anything we do whether as a business executive or housewife (househusband) becomes an opportunity to be of service. Thinking about the times when I began an activity with a heartfelt connection that gave way to other priorities and kept me from being of service was a sobering experience. For example:

- Getting my spouse and/or children to do what I wanted became more important than meeting their needs.
- Making a point became more important than really hearing another.
- Making a profit became more important than caring about the lives of my clients and employees or about the well-being of the environment.
- Giving information became more important than teaching my students to love learning.
- Winning took precedence over the self-esteem of others.

Some of the most challenging issues that I confront on my journey of being more of service include learning more about:

- how serving the highest needs of others is the way I best nurture myself;
- the difference between serving and enabling others;
- how to set and maintain boundaries so my integrity is not compromised.

> **LB:** *I am not creative because I am not artistic.*
> **EB:** *Creativity comes in many different forms and shapes.*

After an absolutely perfect Thanksgiving dinner, my host suggested we play Pictionary. I had never played the game. Reading the rules and knowing that I couldn't draw worth a lick, I declined and offered to be just a spectator. When sides were chosen, there was an uneven number of players. So Alan unilaterally decided that I would be on his team.

I tried hard, but I could not reproduce even the simplest objects. As our team got further and further behind, Alan, a very competitive person, got more and more upset. His irritation did not help. Even though everyone else tried to make lighthearted fun, Alan just got more verbal with his frustration.

Not only will I never play that game again, but also just looking at it on a game shelf sends my stomach into a knot.

For me, creativity had a very narrow definition. Only those who could do things like painting, dancing, or singing were creative artists. Shooting basketballs into a hoop or rolling a ball down an alley definitely did not meet that definition.

My definition expanded a little when someone pointed out that I was really good at connecting people. That was just something I loved to do; it had never seemed like a creative talent. Some people even suggested that I should find a way to make money in connecting people.

It was always a mystery to me why most people never made the connections that I did until I realized that our brains are wired differently. Some people can see an object and reproduce it better than others. Some have better singing voices than others. Some are more athletic. Some have higher IQs. Some have better memories, and some see connections that others do not.

At first, even writing did not seem creative. I got no sense of being creative when an editor was needed to rewrite every sentence. One of the factors that made writing with Margie so unpleasant was how we approached the writing process. I would go over and over sentences until I was happy with how they sounded. Constantly making changes would drive her nuts. She just wanted to get it done and off to the editor.

All that changed when I wrote my first book by myself without even a professional content editor. I found working for hours sculpting a paragraph with new and interesting ways to say things exhilarating. I also discovered that I liked and was good at creating interesting paragraph headings and book titles. I liked pushing the envelope in the ways that I thought and that most people thought. I began to think that, with an expanded definition, I was pretty creative after all.

{ CHAPTER 7 }

# PHYSICAL EVOLUTION:
## My Body Is a Sacred Temple

"Tonight, I'm going to make dinner," I announced three weeks after we'd met.

"I'd love it," she said. "Let's do the shopping together."

I had already planned the menu—one of my special meal-in-itself salads. With Margie in tow, I zipped to the salad dressing section and routinely put a bottle in the shopping cart.

She took it out, put it back on the shelf, and picked out another one, announcing, "This one is better for you."

"Wait a minute. That's my favorite salad dressing, and I don't even know if I'll like this one."

"Just read the labels. Your salad dressing is full of chemicals, and this one doesn't have any," she said.

> **LB:** *There is not much difference in foods.*
> **EB:** *Eating healthy foods is just as easy as eating foods that have questionable health value.*

Uh oh. I knew a health food nut when I saw one. My mother had always been concerned about eating the right foods. She wouldn't buy white bread, and we had liver once a week for dinner. A liver sandwich on whole wheat bread became the symbol of my fight against those who were out to deprive me of hot dogs and ice cream sodas. Now, after six years of freedom, I was face to face with another nut.

Margie and I stalled in front of the salad dressings. Putting her bottle back and recovering my original choice, I said, "I don't believe in any of that stuff." We moved on.

When I took a loaf of bread from the shelf she said, "That bread is awful."

*Here we go again*, I thought."

"Do you know what they put in white bread?" I don't remember answering that question, but she went on anyway. "They take out all the nutrition and substitute chemicals." She was adamant now.

Even more aggravating, she seemed to know what she was talking about. I felt my salad dressing and white bread slipping away. "Okay, I'm not going to argue with you. I'll make you a deal. I'll go along with your food nuttiness, but I will not eat anything that I don't like just because it's good for me."

"That's fine with me, but promise me one thing."

"What's that?"

"That you'll read a book that I'll give you so you can learn something about food."

"It's a deal."

She was tough but reasonable. We could disagree and still get along. My hope she hated liver was dashed. But ground up with stewed onions and schmaltz (okay, no schmaltz, just olive oil), it tasted pretty good.

I have learned to eat more healthfully, and thankfully as the years have gone on, the healthy food section of every market has gotten larger, tastier, and more reasonably priced.

> **LB:** *It is important to finish everything on my plate.*
> **EB:** *Conscious eating means not eating past the point of feeling full and satisfied.*

Growing up, I heard more times than I care to remember, "Finish your plate. There are children starving in Europe."

I internalized that message and got it in spades. I would not only eat everything on my plate but also finish up any leftovers on other people's plates. Stuffed, I would push away from the table. And then one night the "children starving in Europe" world came crashing down.

I was out to dinner with Geneen Roth, a dear friend who writes books about eating healthfully. Geneen had recently finished writing *Breaking Free from Compulsive Eating*. Since I had not read the book, we talked about it as we ate.

We ordered some lovely and not inexpensive food. Being a good boy, I finished mine. She left half of hers. I looked lustfully at the tasty food as the waiter whisked it away. We talked about the food going to waste. She said that she was full and felt fine leaving it.

We left the restaurant and were walking along Pico Boulevard when Geneen spied an ice cream store. "Would you like to stop for some ice cream?"

There is nothing I love more than ice cream. We hurriedly turned left into the shop. Exiting the store lapping up our delicious treat, we continued our walk. I had about four or five bites from my cone when she asked, "Do you feel satisfied?"

I thought for a moment and said, "Yes, I do."

Geneen took the cone out of my hand and threw it in a trashcan by the curb. Flabbergasted, I dove into the trashcan attempting to save my half-eaten treasure. I failed. With a disapproving look and tone I said, "You can't throw away a perfectly good ice cream cone."

"Why not?" she shot back. "You said you felt satisfied."

We continued walking and talking about food and the problems of eating past the point of what my body wanted and needed.

I realized that in addition to my childhood message about starving children, my eating habits were based on what I needed at an earlier time in my life. As I got older, the amount of food I needed was much smaller than when I was still growing or even as a young adult. And yet I continued to order and eat as if I was sixteen years old.

Since that night, I have made some new habits, including ordering less food, taking home half of what I order, or if I am out with a friend, splitting a dinner. Conscious eating has left me nourished both physically and emotionally, as well as kept my weight in the healthy zone.

I can't say that I never eat past the point of feeling full and satisfied or that I never finish another person's plate or that I always eat healthfully. But that scene of diving into the trashcan has remained emblazoned in my conscious since that day thirty years ago.

> **LB:** *There is something wrong with the way my body looks.*
> **EB:** *The way my body naturally looks is perfect.*

From the first day we met, I loved everything about her physically—her face, her hair, and her body. I loved looking at her whenever she stood naked in front of our bathroom mirror.

While I was admiring her entire body, I would notice that her eyes were always looking down at her stomach. When she saw me looking at her, she would close the bathroom door.

When I questioned her about it, she said, "I hate the way my body looks."

"I know your stomach doesn't look the same as it did BC (before children), but I think your body is perfect."

We talked lots about body image and especially about the woman's curse of having to have the "perfect" body.

As I began seeing women differently, I realized the myriad of shapes and sizes that are normal and how my upbringing had focused my thinking in a narrow vein. I also realized that when the body is taken care of and treated respectfully with proper nutrition, regular exercise, and conscious eating habits (like not eating more than we need), every body assumes its natural shape.

A healthy body is something of beauty that I enjoy looking at, whether it is my lover, Michelangelo's *David*, or the nudes of Peter Paul Rubens.

> **LB:** *Exercise occurs as a natural part of life, and I do not need to pay attention to it.*
> **EB:** *The only way I get enough exercise is by making it a ritual.*

I want to die healthy! The thought of wasting away by being overweight and suffering through multiple surgeries like my father and being a costly burden on my family and society is unacceptable. With that as a goal, I do everything I can to avoid illnesses that are within my ability to control.

Getting enough exercise is within my control. In earlier times, between physical labor and walking, people naturally got enough exercise at work or in taking care of a home and garden.

Early in life I got plenty of exercise. Then hip and back problems ended my basketball and tennis days. About that time, I moved to Aspen. Living in a town where exercise was a way of life was breathtaking (the scenery wasn't bad either). Everyone I knew was out biking, hiking, skiing, and walking all the time. As a result, the only overweight people I saw were tourists.

In the summer, I either walked or rode my bike into town and along the many wonderful bike trails. In winter, I was on the ski slopes or walked to downtown. I amazed myself in how much I was able to do. The first time, actually every time, I rode up to Maroon Bells or Ashcroft was a great feeling of accomplishment.

The hour-and-a-half ride from 7,900 feet to 12,000 feet was really difficult, but I did it. After walking around or sitting by Maroon Lake or eating at the Pine Creek Cookhouse, the thirty-minute downhill brought out many whoops and hollers.

I never quite finished the ride all the way up to Independence Pass, the highest paved pass in North America. But halfway up, I stopped at the grottos. The rock formations and ice caves at the grottos were a thrill every time I got there.

Coming back to earth (at least to sea level) and the more sedentary lifestyle of my friends has not been conducive to maintaining the outdoor, physically active life that I once had. I sit a lot in front of my computer or television. I have trouble walking because of hip problems.

So four or five days a week, even though I try to avoid it, I eventually get on my treadmill for a forty-minute workout. I watch the news and try to not think about my tiredness or any of my physical pains. I lose myself in the emotional pain and anger of watching my country disintegrate. I do find a great deal of satisfaction in taking some control over the slow disintegration of an aging body.

So far, so good. I don't know how many more years of being free of serious, debilitating, chronic illness I have. But until the inevitable happens, I'm sure going to do everything I can to keep healthy this sacred temple with which I have been entrusted.

{ CHAPTER 8 }

# SOCIAL EVOLUTION:
## My World Is Our World and Welcome to It

I CAME OF AGE IN THE 1950S. Although my family had always voted Democrat, we were not involved in politics. And then, at a time when great change was starting to disquiet our country, I married into a family that had always been passionately and actively involved in politics.

The day President John F. Kennedy was assassinated changed my rather insulated world forever. It was one of those moments forever emblazoned in my brain. I was standing in line at a bank when the news came across the television. I immediately left the line and rushed home. Margie was watching the news. As the events unfolded before our astonished eyes, we held each other tightly and cried. Nothing like this had ever happened in our lifetimes. A fire was lit.

> **LB:** *The world outside my family does not affect my personal well-being.*
> **EB:** *The one, our unique identity, is constantly in relationship to the many, our community.*

A few years later, another event rocked my world when it touched me directly. President Lyndon Johnson was at the Century City hotel to give a speech. A large demonstration of protesters against the war in Vietnam gathered in front of the hotel. Margie and I were right at the front of the line with our one-year-old son in a stroller. The police in riot gear stood eye to eye inches away from us, pounding their nightsticks into the palms of their hands.

As the crowd grew larger, the tension started building. Margie said, "We've got to get out of here!"

I shot back, "Don't be silly. Nothing is going to happen."

"Listen, we've got a baby here, and we've got to go!"

"Okay," I said sullenly.

We turned and started walking away. We had gone about fifty yards when we heard a commotion. As we turned back we saw the police coming through the crowd smashing heads and bodies with their nightsticks. We walked even faster, thankful we had heeded Margie's intuition and left the scene.

In the next few years, my fire grew larger. A greater awareness of injustices and learning more about our deteriorating environment led to becoming passionately involved in many issues. In addition to the continuing unnecessary war in Vietnam, the issues roiling our world included women clamoring for their right to be treated equally, greater awareness of food being processed in unhealthy ways, global warming, minorities wanting the rights they are constitutionally and morally guaranteed, and students demanding a more meaningful education.

During my employment as the director of program development for a small college, I was charged with developing a program to connect our college with the neighboring community. I jumped into learning a lot about communities.

An important part of that learning centers on how to develop what Mark Gerzon termed global intelligence, or GQ. Gerzon is the founder of Mediators Foundation, convener of cross-party conversation, and author of many books including, *Leading Through Conflict*. He says:

> When knowledge comes from the heart, a community is guided by an intelligence that uses *all* relevant faculties to act effectively across borders. In the kind of communities for which we so deeply yearn, GQ is used in the interest of the whole. Community members, actively in-service, are committed to something larger than self and personal interest.
>
> Members are energetically engaged in furthering the well-being of others. They support each other in

connecting to their hearts. People develop their networking abilities so that they help each other connect to resources that help further both their careers and personal development.

We naturally gravitate to communities that support our journey toward a more satisfying life. Being around people who freely give, and are open to receiving, information and support, fulfills us. Trying to manipulate people into spending time together with guilt or threats does not occur when a heart magnet permeates a community.

Developing safe and empowered communities became a focus of my life. From the largest to the smallest communities, we are all connected. I am affected by and affect others in my family, workplace, city, country, and world. My world is our world.

> **LB:** *Being part of a community meets my need for togetherness.*
> **EB:** *Being meaningfully together meets a deeper need.*

Typical conversations about sports, weather, politics, food, wine, gossip, and past events do not energize me. Spending time in small talk is not wrong or bad, but even though I may be physically close with others, I often feel disconnected and separate.

People seldom share their deepest feelings, needs, or fears. Families may share a meal together but not share their personal concerns. Couples may engage in the most physically intimate act of having sex yet feel a million miles away from each other. People may spend eight hours a day with fellow workers or live only a short distance from their neighbors next door but never really get to know them.

Expressing myself in conversations that are honest and personal connects me to feel appreciation for others and myself. They may be discussions that lead to new discoveries, intimate personal sharing, or learning about what blocks our heartfelt feelings. Such interactions involve being emotionally touched with important personal learning and feeling seen, heard, and appreciated. For example, at mealtimes, discussions

about how we are feeling about our lives and our real concerns hold sway over criticism, arguments, and dispassionate chronologies about the day's events.

With an intention to make heartfelt connections an important and integral part of a community, any activity is an opportunity to be meaningfully together, whether it is parenting, working, volunteering, shopping, lovemaking, eating, or playing.

Learning and being of service provides a compelling reason to meet together. It is the heart of a community and a foremost criterion in determining where and with whom I choose to work, live, and spend time.

> **LB:** *More is better.*
> **EB:** *Simplicity is a key to my happiness.*

Growing up in a bustling metropolis definitely met my need for a stimulating community. In Los Angeles, I thrived in the wealth of consciousness and thinking beyond the norm. However, the inaccessibility due to urban sprawl and overly scheduled lives left me feeling anonymous and isolated. People typically made dates to see each other two or three weeks in advance, met for lunch or dinner, and then did not see each other again for months. Maintaining friendships was a chore.

When I moved to a small town, that all changed dramatically. It was here that I connected to the earth and to people in an entirely new way. The rear balcony of my condo overhung the Roaring Fork River (named for the roar that occurred every spring as it swelled from the snowmelt). My front balcony looked directly out at Aspen Mountain. Right outside my bedroom window stood an aspen tree. I never closed my bedroom curtains so that every morning I could marvel at the tree traveling through its exquisite journey. I watched in awe as its branches went from being draped in a snow-white cover to birthing petite buds that grew into leaves of delicate light green, turned emerald, then quaking gold, and finally left a barren tree awaiting its fresh white cover.

In my new community, making friends was easy, and keeping up those friendships occurred naturally. I was constantly bumping into people I knew walking in town, at restaurants, in movie theaters, or on the ski slopes. It was like being on a college campus. I discovered and evolved a gregarious part of myself that I never knew existed. I loved it!

I lived at a slower pace that allowed for the space that used to exist naturally within extended families, neighborhoods, and schools. In the free-flowing time of just hanging out together, the magic of openhearted engagement often happened. Long, slow dinners, walks in the park, and even doing chores together allowed space and time for the important concerns and questions that surfaced in relaxed interactions.

For many people, that kind of space has given way to overstressed and overworked parents, grandparents who live too far away to be regularly available, unknown neighbors, and speedy transportation that whisks us past each other, as well as past any natural beauty that may have survived our advancing civilization.

In addition, modern technology that allows communication to take place without ever having to meet face to face and heart to heart threatens to complete our headlong rush into isolation and alienation. Even when parents make great efforts to spend quality time with their children, the demands of professional careers, earning enough money to insure a quality life for their children, and attending to their personal needs make unstructured, relaxed time a rare commodity.

I have come to greatly appreciate the importance of living simply. Living a simpler life, although simple, is not easy. The constant beat from advertisers promises that happiness, success, and satisfaction come from accumulating things. However, looking around at the people who have attained everything that is supposed to make them happy, it is hard not to think, "What's wrong with this picture?" Living lighter and more trouble-free may not be good for the nation's economy, but it is good for me.

In an economy that is based on creating beliefs that our unhappiness is because we do not have enough of something, living with a lighter touch may seem downright un-American. I do not own a big house, a late-model car, or lots of clothes and jewelry, do not go out to fancy restaurants, and do not indulge in expensive entertainment or recreational activities. I do have time to connect with nature, friends, and myself while walking and allowing conversations to wind into deep and wonderful places.

In giving up a lifestyle in which I accumulated many wonderful things, I have substituted the freedom of not having to support those things. I do not have to work long hours and have evolved into living simply rich. This requires letting go of what is unnecessary. It means living with less—less debt, less clutter, fewer things that break down, and fewer people for whom I take responsibility. The goal is to create less stress and greater equanimity and leave more time to enjoy the gifts that life has given me, such as nature and family.

Living lightly includes keeping things in a perspective that allows for serious discussions without taking things too seriously. Such a perspective is reflected in the Buddhist saying, "Act always as if the future of the Universe depends on what you do, while laughing at yourself for thinking that whatever you do makes any difference."

> **LB:** *I can't dance.*
> **EB:** *Dancing that I can do and enjoy embraces moving to the rhythm of the music that touches my heart.*

At the beginning chapter 6, I mentioned growing up in a home with a professional dancer who was out-of-this-world fabulous, I considered dancing to be moving in prescribed ways and a women's thing. Knowing I couldn't dance and not wanting to look foolish, I avoided dancing like the plague. I would never even move to music.

One cold November night, my neighborhood theatre was hosting a film festival. I had never heard of the film for the evening, *Strictly Ballroom*. I asked the person sitting next to me if she knew what the film was about. She said that all she knew was that it was an Australian farce about ballroom dancing.

I didn't think it was the kind of film I would enjoy. But what the heck, the theatre was packed with people most of whom I knew, and the after party was sure to be a hoot.

Watching the film boggled my mind. Something about the sound and rhythms of the music touched me in a way that I had never experienced. I could not stop smiling, and my body seemed to have a mind of its own as I danced in my seat.

As the credits rolled, I got up with everyone else in the theatre and, spontaneously moving to the music, filed out of the theatre. I said to myself, *That was so much fun. I want to do it some more!*

When friends invited me to join them in a dance class they were taking, I tentatively accepted their invitation. The next day I bought some dance CDs and began listening. Before ever attending my first class, I found myself hooked on ballroom dance music. I had it constantly playing on my stereo. Rather than walking from room to room, I danced my way across my apartment.

The music connected to an unexplored and unknown part of me. It brought my sensual feelings closer to the surface and allowed me to laugh and cry more easily.

Getting out of my head and into my heart felt wonderful, indulgent, and romantic. I thought, *I don't know if this is what it means to be out of my mind or if that is what I was frightened of, but I love it.*

I couldn't get enough dance talk with my friends. One evening we got together for dinner and to watch the film *Tango*. We were mesmerized. I gushed, "That was the most stunningly gorgeous film I have ever seen!"

"Yeah, the dancing was amazing, but the lighting and the costumes were incredible," Marla added. "I can't wait for our class."

My first night in class exceeded my expectations. Jeff, the teacher, was affable, encouraging, and very accepting. He began by saying, "For me, dancing is very basic and simple. It is letting the rhythm move your body. Partnership dancing is doing that with someone else. Connection happens when your heart is involved in this process. That's what this class will be all about."

My mind immediately recalled one of my favorite scenes from *Strictly Ballroom* when the grandmother asks the hotshot dancer, "Where do you feel the rhythm?" He replies by moving his feet.

Grandma stops him, cups her hands over his chest, and begins alternately beating out a cadence as she says, "Here and here." After a few beats, she says, "Listen to the rhythm. Don't be scared."

I smiled, feeling as if I was in heaven. All I had been hungering for was epitomized in the dancing. Dancing and music became vehicles for opening my heart and connecting to joy, the feeling that is so nourishing. Whereas in the past I could nurture others, now I was still learning new ways to nurture myself.

I would not call myself a great dancer. But I'm pretty darn good, and whenever I allow myself to be moved physically and emotionally, it feels creative and very fulfilling.

{ Chapter 9 }

# Childhood Evolution:
## It's Never Too Late to Recapture My Heart and Have a Happy Childhood

Continuing to evolve beyond my Limiting Beliefs and developing more of my potential has brought me full circle. With the wisdom and maturity of an adult and the innocence and spontaneity of childhood, I experience riches beyond belief.

> **LB:** *Being an adult is serious business and means not being childlike.*
> **EB:** *Childlike play and a sense of humor are my birthright.*

My friendship with Lee encouraged me to recapture parts of myself that got lost in my headlong rush into adulthood. One of these was my ability to play and have fun. I had become a very serious, "nose to the grindstone," responsible, and productive kind of guy.

Lee, on the other hand, was my first male friend who had developed and balanced the many sides of himself. He was a successful businessman and a creative artist, a skilled athlete and very sensitive. He was an intellectual who was very comfortable playing naturally and non-competitively and not afraid of looking foolish.

One day while walking along a snow-covered trail, Lee fell into the snow and spontaneously began laughing, screaming, and rolling down the hill. When he got to the bottom he yelled, "What are you waiting for?"

I gulped and launched myself into the snowbank, tumbling down toward him as he waited, snowball in hand. We ran and threw snowballs until we collapsed giggling in a heap. "You're pretty good at this!" Lee chided.

I grinned, "That was really fun. I haven't done anything like that since I was a kid."

"Well, when you let go," Lee took a breath and, calling up his best Forrest Gump imitation, continued, "It's like a box of chocolates. You never know what you're going to get. Sometimes it's magic. There certainly are no guarantees, but it's always an adventure." As I looked in awe at this Yoda in front of me, I was filled with gratitude for the perfection of this moment.

Our "magical mystery tour" extended into everything we did. At parties, I allowed myself to dance freely, giving my body permission to gyrate in ways that felt connected to my internal rhythm. Biking, hiking, listening to concerts, watching sunsets and sunrises, looking at the stars, having philosophical discussions, and reading poetry all flowed easily, sometimes in tears and sometimes in laughter.

One evening, I met a woman at a party, and in the course of the evening, she said, "I never heard a man giggle before."

I thought for a moment and then replied, "I never giggled before I moved here, and I love it."

Meeting O. Fred Donaldson was another experience that helped me recapture the joy of childhood. Donaldson is a researcher who has been studying play for over forty years. He has written about what he calls "original play" in his book, *Playing by Heart*. The following describes my experience in one of Donaldson's workshops and illustrates what childlike play looks and feels like.

I felt really odd and nervous entering a room full of strangers who were going to learn about play. But Donaldson immediately put us at ease. On his tee shirt were the words, "You don't quit playing because you get old. You get old because you stop playing." With his soft manner and entertaining stories, he masterfully created a safe environment.

For the first couple of hours, we just talked, asked questions, and practiced some of Donaldson's exercises for understanding original play. This is the egoless, non-self-conscious kind of play that we knew as children before our ideas about play became contaminated with rules, expected outcomes, or the need to win.

In original play, there are no demands, attempts to get one's desires met, tickling, or grabbing. When he thought we were ready to engage in original play, he said we were going to get down on the floor and play as puppies and kittens. He told those of us who felt more comfortable with more energetic play to go to one end of the room and those who wanted a slower play to go to the other end. I chose the slower end.

As people came together, I closed my eyes and just allowed my body to blend into the pile of people next to me, under me, and on top of me. The pile seemed to assume an identity of its own. We seemed to be dancing to some undetermined rhythm—sometimes together, other times apart.

In the spontaneous flow of moving together and apart, there was an openness that brought forth receptivity, spontaneity, and a sensitivity that heightened the awareness of what each other needed. When someone started to laugh, the laughter spread to others and quickly engulfed the room. The rest of our time together was just pure, unadulterated fun.

When I stop worrying about how I'm coming across and just react, I find humor everywhere. My voice is not level and controlled. My body is not stiff and tense. I'm loose and expressive. I'm on an arm-swinging, free-wheeling, natural high.

Maintaining a sense of humor requires seeing the lighter side of things. Heartfelt humor is gentle, playful, respectful, life-affirming, and clean. It cannot be cruel or disrespectful, as is sarcasm. Sarcastic remarks are covert expressions of anger often covering an intent to control another person.

Light-hearted talk adds to my fun in many ways. Whether loving words or trashy talk, it is never sexist or critical. Sometimes, I might share what I think is fun or funny, and another person has a negative reaction or admits to his or her shyness or inhibitions. Should that happen, as with any other upset, I have a choice. I can close my heart and begin a potential argument, become silently distant, or embrace the difficulty as another opportunity for learning and creating even greater closeness.

Heartfelt fun flows with a light-hearted energy. Such a mood encourages a heightening of my senses. The heaviness that surrounded an overly burdened me made that kind of fun a rare event.

Not taking things so seriously allows experiencing a great deal more from every situation. Matthew Fox, founder of the University of Creation Spirituality, said in *The Coming of the Cosmic Christ*, "In allowing one's authentic awe and wonder to be born again and in welcoming the child and playfulness, to come to self-expression, one is already involved in co-creation. For there is no creation without play. The Cosmic Christ is a comic Christ with a sense of humor."

To remind myself that life is not intended to be such a serious affair, I think back to the countless number of times I became upset with something. I remember getting upset—about another person being late, a child spilling a glass of milk, a lover's rejection, a disappointment over my expectations not being met, how I looked physically—only to think sometime later, *Why did I make such a big deal over that? It doesn't seem very important right now.*

The title of Richard Carlson's book, *Don't Sweat the Small Stuff . . . and It's All Small Stuff*, says it all. Sometimes, lightening up with a sense of humor even in the most difficult situations helps keep things in perspective.

> **LB:** *I need to be with other people to have fun.*
> **EB:** *I can have fun by myself.*

Children have an uncanny ability of getting totally immersed in doing something by themselves. Surprisingly, some of my most important lessons about creating my own sense of fun and well-being came from skiing.

I had come to Aspen determined to become a better skier. I worked hard and braved many miserably cold days to improve. But one day as Lee and I were talking about having fun, I realized that I wasn't having fun skiing. "What's missing?" I asked. "What do you get out of skiing?"

Lee thought for a moment and said, "You know, I used to be obsessed with my technique just like you. But one day I was skiing by myself. It was a glorious, crystal-clear, sparkling day, and I got into just connecting with all of nature's grandeur and perfection—the majesty of the mountains, the purity of the snow, the deep blue of the sky. It was a spiritual experience. Since then, no matter what the technical level of my skiing, I enjoy nothing more than my time on the slopes."

The next day, I had a leisurely breakfast, got to the mountain at 10:00 a.m. instead of my usual 8:30, and skied with an entirely different orientation. It was sensational. At the end of the day when I met Lee in the Jacuzzi, I was beaming. "You know," I said, hardly able to contain my excitement, "today I learned how skiing alone can be very satisfying.

"But I also realized that when you and I ski together, it's also fun and satisfying because of our rides together up the chairlift, our lunches on the mountain, and our stopping and chatting during our runs. I'm really excited by what a difference it would make anytime I go skiing with another person if I made connecting with that person and having fun the primary reasons I was out on the slopes."

Skiing became one of my favorite ways to have fun and connect deeply to myself and to others. When I was connected in this way, my sense of well-being soared. I eagerly looked forward to skiing dates as times when I could spend time with friends without the usual distractions of life. Even the days when the chairlift got stuck and we dangled high above the ground were opportunities to connect and so became enjoyable.

One day while having lunch at Ruthie's restaurant, watching the skiers glide downhill, and greeting friend after friend, I thought, *I know many of my old friends would never believe this, but when I connect with myself and nature, skiing is just as good as having sex. Wow, what a concept! I had better keep this one just between Lee and myself.*

Learning to create my own sense of well-being allowed for a freedom I had never imagined possible. Lee and I developed a relationship that incorporated many wonderful aspects of true friendship. We established a deep emotional and spiritual bond without imposing any restrictions on the other.

This was illustrated one Fourth of July when we were cruising Main Street during the holiday parade. At noon, under a cloudless cerulean sky, began the corny, yet always wonderful, hometown extravaganza featuring a procession of dogs wearing western bandannas, a cavalcade of floats and marching bands, and the volunteer fire department driving their engines while throwing candy to the kids.

Everyone was having a great time, and it was people at their best. Lee and I wanted to soak up every connection we could make. As we wove through the crowd, we stopped every few feet to talk with friends. We were totally in our element, having great fun enjoying ourselves and enjoying each other.

We'd gotten half way up Main Street when the float of the Aspen Kayak School stopped in front of us. Lee spotted it and spontaneously began running toward the float, yelling to me, "I want to ride in the kayak. I'll catch up with you later."

As Lee climbed into the kayak on top of the float and began laughing with his kayaking buddies and kibitzing with friends on the sidewalk, I was delighted and continued my journey.

Hours later, we rendezvoused near the end of the parade route. We shared our experiences as we walked toward the Cantina restaurant for some refreshments. I talked about how different it felt being able to support someone making a spontaneous decision to change plans.

I said, "In the past, if someone had done something like that, I would have been upset. When we'd have gotten back together, for me to teach a lesson about never breaking an agreement or disappointing me, I probably would have been cold and withdrawn. It would have been an awful reunion. Instead, you and I just pick up where we leave off and continue having a wonderful time."

Lee smiled, "You know, if I ever thought that something like that would be really difficult for you, we'd talk about it. But knowing you'll have a great time whether I'm there or not really frees me. I love that part of our relationship. Do you think it's possible to have that kind of freedom in a committed relationship with a woman?"

"Hmmm," I replied, "I don't know, but I sure hope so." Later that evening in the crystal clear altitude of eight thousand feet, the vivid colors of the fireworks display and sparkling lights exploding in concert with my favorite selections of classical music moved me to tears. That was the dessert course for the most incredible holiday celebration I had ever had.

> **LB:** *The guilt from all the unloving things I have done is a burden I must bear.*
> **EB:** *Given my Limiting Beliefs and fears at any moment in time, I am always doing the best that I can and things could not have been any different.*

This Evolving/Empowering Belief, which was referred to in chapter 3, frees my childlike consciousness from the suffocation of guilt and is worth repeating and remembering.

Knowing this does not take away the existential sadness over how much more loving and meaningful our lives together would have been had my Evolving/Empowering Beliefs been present. I would have been less **fear full** and more:

- **heart full** in sharing everything with you;
- **feeling full** in engaging with you;
- **faith full** in allowing you to unfold, rather than trying to control things and get my way;
- **joy full** in participating in the lighter side of things and laughing more;
- **tear full** in expressing my sensitive nature;
- **care full** in attending to your pain and needs;
- **play full** in having fun together;
- **peace full** in reacting to life's vicissitudes;
- **grace full** in dancing through our life together;
- **delight full** in sharing our good fortunes;
- **mind full** in attending to your needs;
- **thought full** in responding to your questions;
- **cheer full** in beginning and ending each day.

As I approach the end of my life cycle, I don't know what's going to happen, and I don't care. If death is an ending, and there is nothing beyond this life, then so be it. If there are lifetimes and reincarnations beyond this life, then my destiny looks quite rosy. So I approach the unknowable without any fear, and that feels so nice.

Since I don't want to end in the void, the following experience lives as a constant reminder of what is possible when fear rides in the backseat while the freedom of childhood drives the car.

## An Adult Happy Childhood Experience

A warm and cloudless day called us to a hike. With backpacks overflowing with goodies and canteens filled with fresh water, we were off on an adventure. We rode bikes to Hunter Creek Trail, locked them to a fence, and began our journey. The fall colors were peaking. Within a few short steps of the trailhead, we stopped on a wooden footbridge spanning the still waters of a shimmering creek. Immersed in an autumn palette of red and brown from the scrub oak mixed with evergreens topped with a clear blue sky, we inhaled the majestic beauty and smells of nature's resplendence. We were transfixed.

The occasional crackling of twigs being broken by an unseen animal punctuated the silence. We hugged each other, and my heart felt like it was about to burst. Gazing deeply into Susan's eyes, I couldn't hold back my tears as we acknowledged our gratitude for this precious time together.

Moving up the trail, we giggled as we climbed over boulders, sloshed through mud, and waded through shallow parts of the creek. Not being on a schedule allowed us the rare experience of wandering. We discovered new colors, found hidden life forms, fed the squirrels that brazenly took food out of our hands, and felt one with nature. We laughed when I expressed the realization that "it was probably necessary to wander in order to find wonder."

When we reached the high meadow at the top of the creek, the entire hillside was covered with trees with multicolored leaves. We sat down to eat lunch amongst this mosaic backdrop. Our noontime show included a family of deer that, although keeping a respectable distance, seemed to be joining us.

After more hiking, playing, and exploring, we headed back down the trail. We started running. Losing my self-consciousness and abandoning any messages that told me to be careful, I blended with the environment. I imagined myself like the Native Americans who had once summered in these mountains.

    I stopped to rest and deeply inhaled the clean mountain air while waiting for Susan. We sat for a long time relating our incredible feelings. We had each experienced losing fear and becoming one with the mountain. With hearts wide open, we joyfully connected with each other as we had with nature and animals.

# Appendix:
## Actions for Moving from Limiting Beliefs to Evolving/Empowering Beliefs

## Preparing to let go of a Limiting Belief

At the top of a blank sheet of paper, write down a Limiting Belief and its opposite Evolving/Empowering Belief. Now write the answers to the following questions:

### 1. How did I get the Limiting Belief?

Where did the belief come from, and why did you adopt it? Did you hear it from one of your close relatives and decide it was the right way to be? Was it taught to you in your religious training or by your peers? Did you get it through books you read or from television programs?

Discovering the source of your beliefs may be interesting, but it is just a starting point. Think of the many beliefs you adopted in childhood that have disappeared. When a belief does not serve some important purpose, you automatically let it go.

### 2. What are the negative consequences of holding the Limiting Belief?

What effect does this belief have on your mental and physical health and on your relationships? To discover more about the protected feelings and behaviors that follow Limiting Beliefs, review the list that follows. If you have difficulty identifying a feeling as protected, put it through the test of whether compassion was predominant and an intent to learn was present.

### 3. What do I fear happening if I let go of the Limiting Belief?

These fears are the very important reasons you have for holding onto the belief, that is, the purpose the belief is now serving.

### 4. What are the positive outcomes of adopting the Evolving/Empowering Belief?

How would you behave and what would result if your heartfelt feelings were operational and you were nurturing the heartfelt feelings of others and yourself? Heartfelt behavior occurs naturally when compassion dominates over fear and you feel self-confident in the faith that, no matter what happens, you will thrive.

**5. What can I do to prepare myself for letting go of the Limiting Belief?**

Evolving past a Limiting Belief requires strengthening both your self-esteem and support system. Very few people ever jump into difficult water without developing their ability to swim and making sure there are people around to help them should they get into trouble.

Perhaps the most important preparation is respecting wherever you are in the exploration process. This means learning to not make yourself wrong during those times when you are disconnected from your heart-felt feelings. Respect that in those moments your usually unconscious intent was to cover up vulnerable feelings and thus protect yourself.

## A Partial List of Heartfelt Feelings and Behaviors

HEARTFELT FEELINGS AND BEHAVIORS are naturally present when not blocked by fear. They are soft and warm and accompanied by an openness to learning.

Heartfelt feelings are: compassion, joy, love, empathy, acceptance, faith, sympathy, sadness, sorrow, contentment, serenity, humility, fulfillment, bliss, innocent, tender, relaxed, peaceful, calm, gentle, harmonious, happy, alive, cheerful, sparkling, vibrant, delighted, enthusiastic, graceful, light, alert, optimistic, blissful, glad, playful, upbeat, animated, ecstasy, excited, happy, passionate, sensual, and freeing.

Heartfelt behaviors are: being of service, crying, laughing, caring, comforting, nurturing, being affectionate, giving, honoring, embracing, forgiveness; reverence, connected, intimate, mindful, appreciative, grateful, considerate, thoughtful, generous, receptive, benevolent, and accepting.

Being open to learning includes: curiosity, concern, inquisitiveness, attentiveness, involvement, and a desire to learn about others and oneself.

# A Partial List of Protective Feelings and Behaviors

Protective feelings and behaviors cover heartfelt feelings and result from the fear of being vulnerable. They are hard and cold, and there is no desire to learn.

Protective manipulative feelings are: annoyance, irritation, belligerence, combativeness, anger, rage, fuming, loathing, hate, fury, hostility, being irate, madness, outrage, pissed off, judging, blaming, condescension, uptightness, exasperation, disgust, bitterness, and hysteria.

Protective disaffected feelings are: envy, greed, alienation, jealousy, spite, resentment, disheartenment, emptiness, boredom, inadequacy, insecurity, distractedness, dissatisfaction, unhappiness, being a victim, guilt, shame, stressing out, grouchiness, despondency, aloneness, separateness, loneliness, disconnectedness, emotional distance, misery, anxiety, and neediness.

Protective behaviors are: arguing, criticism, revenge, cruelty, quarrelsomeness, ridiculing, demeaning, yelling, hitting, lecturing, controlling, whining, and shaming; attempting to convince, convert, win over, prove a point, impose guilt, get something, and be understood; threatening and/or carrying out threats; telling others how and what they should be feeling and/or doing; avoidance; withdrawing into indifference; giving the silent treatment; and imprisoning.

## Recentering

When in a protective interaction, we often get so caught up in it that we are unaware we are even in it. Therefore, in recentering yourself, becoming more aware is essential in both beginning and ending this exercise. Here are all seven steps.

1. **Awareness** – Become aware that you are protective and you are jailed in protective interactions. If you are unsure about being protected, check out "A Partial List of Protective Feelings and Behaviors" on the previous page, and see if you are protected.

2. **Disengage** – If you are protected and wish to recenter yourself, then disengage from the interaction. This means stopping any attempts to convince the other person that he or she is wrong or to see things differently.

3. **Cleanse** – Get the cold, hard defensiveness out of your body. Taking a few deep breaths will often work. When that is not enough, you might need to take the time to get recentered.

4. **Recenter** – Find a quiet place to meditate, write out your thoughts and feelings, listen to some peaceful music, or engage in some physical activity. Try the following meditation:

    - Breathe deeply and visualize how you look and feel as a secure, open, and loving person.

    - Recall times when you were connected to the best place inside of you, when you felt content and proud of who you are with nothing to hide and nothing to prove. Such experiences may have occurred in nature or during your everyday activities.

5. **Learn** – You are connected to your heart when warm feelings are present and you are open to learning about both the other person and yourself. When that happens, think about and write down what you learned regarding your part of the difficulty, that is, how you were interacting.

6. **Engage** – You might want to return to the situation. Or not. If you return to the situation with heartfelt feelings, you might start out the conversation by making amends for your part in the difficulty. If your partner is open to learning, your interaction will be a positive one.

7. **Awareness** – To the best of your ability stay checked in to your body. If your partner or you are not open to learning, you will feel sad and scared. If so, you need to take care of yourself in some way.

    If you hope to get your partner to change and/or learn something, then you are not open to learning. You are in the jail of a protected interaction. You can get out of jail and go directly to step 1. Or you can stay in jail, keep fighting, and hope for a different outcome.

Are we having fun yet?

## Unblocking Compassionate Forgiveness

Whenever compassionate forgiveness is blocked, I begin moving forward by first making it acceptable that I am not able to do it. Then I can learn what is blocking my compassionate forgiveness.

For example, I may discover the fear that if I feel compassion, I will be more vulnerable to being taken advantage of. If this is the case, I can respect the fact that until I have more confidence in my ability to set boundaries, my self-protecting behavior is necessary.

When I give myself this acceptance, I feel content and more ready to take the next step, which might entail understanding more about what it means to set boundaries without losing my compassion. Whenever I do not respect my self-protectiveness, I can learn what is blocking that acceptance.

## Recognizing How Rigidly Held Beliefs Affect Your Life

1. Write a belief you hold for which there is no universal agreement or factual proof that it is the truth.

2. Do you really believe it to be an incontrovertible fact? If your answer is yes, go directly to #5. If your answer is no, go to #3.

3. Do other people think you believe it is a fact? (You can check it out by asking friends and family.)

4. If most people believe you believe it, you can learn about the things you may be doing that give your utterances such definitiveness. If people give you authority and power, ask them about your part in creating a system that disempowers them and blocks fulfilling connections. Ask them about your body language (facial expressions, tightness in your arms and torso), tone of voice, and defensiveness. Become more introspective and aware of any internal tension and hardness that may close off your learning.

5. What are the results of holding a belief rigidly with people who do not believe as you do? How do people react—for example, argumentatively, compliantly, or judgmentally? How do you feel about the lack of hear-learning discussions that result?

6. What do you fear happening if you hold a belief as a personal truth and a choice rather than as a fact? For example, you may fear being mistaken and unlovable, out of control, left adrift, rejected, or lonely. Or you may fear being unable to maintain the belief because it would not have authority and that just believing it because it feels good and you like it may not be enough. If that is so, what might happen then?

## Respectful Behavior

*Honoring.* Being aware of and considering other people's boundaries—their right not to have anything done to them that they do not want done or that violates their sensitivities.

*Accepting.* Appreciating differences by valuing and supporting the choices and feelings of others.

*Empathetic Feedback.* Feedback that acknowledges and understands the feelings of others. It follows from knowing that all behavior is motivated by important reasons.

*Being Inclusive.* Inviting others to participate in discussions and decisions about things that affect them.

*Cooperation.* Considering and valuing each person's thoughts and feelings when working on tasks and goals.

*Faith.* Maintaining one's caring while allowing others to solve their own problems, especially in the face of difficulties.

*Humility.* Remaining unattached to beliefs. Having strong ideas but holding them lightly enough to remain open and flexible.

*Open to Learning.* Desiring to learn about oneself and others when differences occur. Having faith that solutions that do not compromise anyone's integrity emerge from exploration and learning.

## Disrespectful Behavior

*Manipulation.* Attempting to control people and things. Not considering what others want, think, or feel, thus violating their physical and/or emotional boundaries.

*Punishing.* Imposing or threatening negative consequences—hitting, yelling, or silence when upset with another.

*Criticizing/Judging.* Making others wrong for their thoughts, feelings, actions, or words. Communicating that another person is stupid, a jerk, crazy, weird, etc.

*Being Unavailable.* Making other things more important than being fully present and really hearing another.

*Egotistical Competition.* Interactions where there is a need to prove something or win at the expense of others.

*Caretaking.* Enabling dependency by taking responsibility for others and continuing to do things for them that they are capable of doing for themselves.

*Unsolicited Sharing.* Expressing feelings or pushing information and advice that has not been asked for and is not wanted.

*Arguing/Debating/Persuading.* Attempts to win, get one's way, be right, or prove a point by convincing others to change their beliefs and behavior.

www.ingramcontent.com/pod-product-compliance
Lightning Source LLC
Chambersburg PA
CBHW052156110526
44591CB00012B/1976